LIKE THE DEER THAT YEARNS

Like the deer that yearns
for running streams
so longs my soul for you, O Lord.

Psalm 42:1

LIKE THE DEER THAT YEARNS

Listening to the Word and Prayer

Edited by
Salvatore A. Panimolle

 St Paul Publications

Original title: *Ascolto della Parola e Preghiera. La* lectio divina. Copyright ©
1987 Libreria Editrice Vaticana, Città del Vaticano

Translated from the Italian by John Glen and Callan Slipper

"The *lectio divina* in the liturgy today: a key to pastoral renewal" by John Glen
is original. Copyright © 1990 St Paul Publications

.

St Paul Publications
Middlegreen, Slough SL3 6BT, England

Copyright © St Paul Publications 1990

Printed by Dotesios Printers Ltd, Trowbridge

ISBN 0 85439 319 6

St Paul Publications is an activity of the priests and brothers of the Society of St
Paul who proclaim the Gospel through the media of social communication

Contents

Introduction

Salvatore A. Panimolle

It is not easy to give a literal translation of the expression *lectio divina*. In the monastic tradition, however, its meaning appears obvious enough. In the rule of St Benedict it is clearly understood to be the reading of the Sacred Scriptures and, together with work and prayer, constitutes one of the three fundamental activities of the monk (Rule 48:1). It is meant to be a careful reading with no view to satisfying intellectual curiosity but rather to nourish the life of faith. The disciple of Benedict must feed each day on this divine food so as to be sustained on what is frequently a difficult and laborious journey. Hence in the Rule, a canonical document imbued with the spirit of the Gospel, the monk is encouraged to listen willingly to the holy readings (*"lectiones sanctas"*).

This reading of the Bible is called "divine" principally because of its object: it is the Word of God, the Holy Book. Yet it also refers to the manner or way in which it is done. For in the *lectio divina* the purpose is not to engage in scholarly pursuits or to do a technical exercise of literary, historical criticism, as Scripture scholars read and study the Bible particularly in modern times. The *lectio divina* has a *vital* and *existential* purpose. It seeks rather to nourish faith, to aid the deepening of a personal relationship with God and his Son.

Hence the inner dispostion with which one engages in the *lectio divina* is not primarily intellectual or scholarly but is rather from the heart's thirst to drink from the living waters of the Word, to satisfy the vital need for happiness and salvation. The term *lectio divina*, therefore, means a *religious* or *dutiful* listening to Scripture, as depicted in the Second Vatican Council's Constitution on Revelation (DV 10). It is a sacred reading (*lectio sacra*), quite distinct from study (DV 25).

Of course the Bible can be read and studied critically, analysing the various problems and themes of this ancient book as one might with any secular document. In our own day this way of proceeding is extremely popular, indeed almost dominant, among professional biblicists. The majority of these employ a whole range of the most up-to-date exegetical techniques to discover the origins or the various strata of literary composition of a text or book in the Bible. They place in high relief the historical forms and the ways in which a biblical passage has been redacted and transmitted. They seek to determine the original meaning of particular sayings or events. They study the proper literary form of pericopes or whole sections in order to work out the particular or collective structure of the passages.

The scholarly approach has its place and importance even when the Bible is read in a faith context. No one today can afford to be totally ignorant of the many complex historical, literary and critical problems associated with this divine book. Clearly, however, the majority of the faithful do not require a high degree of scholarship to be able to read Holy Scripture. Nonetheless, it is extremely desirable, if not indispensable, to be aware of the main conclusions of such technical studies. One can use good, even though rather staid, introductions to the various books of the Bible, using explanatory notes to understand the more difficult passages. It is also extremely helpful to use theological and pastoral commentaries which illuminate the meaning, doctrine and message of biblical writings. There are today a wide selection of such theological, pastoral and spiritual commentaries prepared by excellent authors. The only difficulty appears to be one of choice.

In the first phase of the *lectio divina*, after having heard the sacred text several times and before going on to the following phase of personal reflection and prayer, it is generally very profitable to read such commentaries and explanatory notes. It helps one grasp the true meaning of the Word and avoid the danger of misunderstanding the divine message. Otherwise we fall into the error of the Monophysites, because we ignore, or even deny, the saving mystery of the Incarnation.

The words of the Bible have taken on human forms, the ways of speaking of a particular historical people and culture, just as the Word was made flesh in Palestine, becoming a member of the Jewish race. The theological saying *"cardo salutis caro"* is also true of Scripture. The divine message can be reached only through the letter and indeed through studying the text carefully. In the same manner that we come to the divinity of Christ and obtain salvation by passing through his humanity, so the true meaning of the written Word can be established through scholarship which is frequently long, difficult and wearisome.

Biblical scholars play a major role insofar as the Word of God is concerned in the Church today, laying their rare and very precious charism at the service of the whole community of believers. They have been encouraged by the Second Vatican Council to continue their ministry with joy and constancy (DV 23). The community of believers is obliged in turn not to waste such a gift of the Spirit, intended for the good of the whole Body of Christ (cf. 1 Cor 12:14), either by ignoring or by refusing to be open to the insights of exegesis. Ordinary Christians are called upon to deepen their biblical culture continually and this applies especially to religious and to catechists. It leads to the sublime knowledge of Jesus Christ, because ignorance of the Scriptures is ignorance of Christ, while familiarity with exegesis, and consequently a deep knowledge of the Word, is conducive to living with the Word, the Saviour of the world (DV 25).

When it comes to *lectio divina*, however, the initial stage of studying the sacred text to grasp its meaning is not done in an irreligious manner, as if one were dealing with a secular book. The believer recognizes that the Bible is a work of divine love. For the Sacred Scripture contains the Word addressed by God the Father to his children, exiles on earth. So the believer will study the Bible within a religious perspective, with devotion and faith: those same dispositions with which the faithful go to the Eucharist to participate in the Supper of the Lord (DV 21).

The *lectio divina* presumes this attitude of faith. Scripture comes from God. It is the Word that the Lord has spoken and continues to speak to his people, so that they may have life and may know the path to follow to attain eternal salvation. For believers the Bible is the book of God. In it the heavenly Father reveals his wonderful plan of love for his sinful children. In it he speaks in ways that are always alive and real to the bride of his Son, stimulating a response of faith, promoting an ever deeper commitment to his saving will, bringing an increase of intimacy, love, knowledge and communion.

Believers come to the Holy Scriptures in order to draw from this well the waters of salvation. They find here answers to the painful questions of human existence. Here they are nourished with bread from heaven as they journey on earth till reaching their heavenly home. It is listening in faith, not a secular way of reading or a mostly scholarly method of research that can resolve critical issues. The *lectio divina* then is a *vital and living way of reading the Word*. It is not something purely intellectual. It embraces all of life and the whole span of human existence in its religious dimension.

The Bible itself speaks of this living and salvific purpose of the Word. The Ten Commandments written upon two tablets of stone were proclaimed by Moses to the people of Israel so that they would know how to observe the covenant they were about to make with the Lord (Ex 24:4ff), and so not only be protected, defended and cared for by this great and terrible God (Ex 34:10ff), but also have life and salvation (Deut 31:10ff; 32:46-47). The reading of the Law after it had been rediscovered in the Temple during the reign of Josiah brought about the religious renewal of the whole people of God (2 Kings 22:3-23.27). Ezra and the Levites' proclamation of the Torah in a language that the assembly could understand transfixed their hearts (Neh 8:1ff).

The reading of the Word is orientated to the attainment of eternal life, following the commandments of the Lord (Lk 10:55ff). Indeed the Jews held that they had God's salvation through the Scriptures (Jn 5:39). Hence every Sabbath they listened to the proclamation of the Mosaic Law and of the writings of the prophets (Lk 4:ff), even when they were not in Palestine (cf. Acts 13:14ff.27; 15:21).

Paul of Tarsus expects the understanding of the mystery of Christ to come from the reading of his letters (Eph 3:4), and consequently he tells his followers to read them with care (1 Thess 5:27; Col 4:16). Since reading the Bible is essential, the minister of the Word must work hard at it, hence Timothy is exhorted by his master: "Attend to the public reading of scripture" (1 Tim 4:13).

A reading of the Bible that affects life profoundly can be done only as a result of the action of the Holy Spirit. He makes his presence felt and awakens and deepens commitment to the Word ever more firmly. A person is born to divine life only through the work of the Spirit who lights up the spark of faith in the heart (cf. Jn 3:3ff) and makes believers into children of God (Jn 1:12; 1 Jn 5:1). For this reason *lectio divina* can be called "spiritual" reading because it is the Holy Spirit who inspires, who gives light to the eyes of the soul, who pulls aside the veil of unbelief so that people may see clearly and grasp the depths of meaning in Holy Scripture (cf. 2 Cor 3:14ff). An authentic reading of the Word comes about in the Spirit, when the heart opens itself to the action of this divine Person who breaks through the crust of unbelief and revives the flame of faith, showing the treasures of divine knowledge and wisdom lying in the pages of the Bible. He is the one who reveals the unfathomable richness of the saving plan of God the Father (cf. Rom 11:33; Col 1:27) contained in Scripture. That is why St Jerome, one of the greatest exegetes of all time and who had a tremendous sensitivity to the problems of biblical scholarship, underlined the important role of the Holy Spirit in understanding the sacred texts correctly (*In Gal.* III, V,19-21).

This living reading of the Bible begins with a prayer to the Holy Spirit and continues in prayer. It turns into loving dialogue with the heavenly Father. It leads to the contemplation of the wonders of the story of salvation culminating in its most expressive form in the incarnation, passion, death, resurrection and ascension of the Son of God. In the passage of St Jerome's letter to the Galatians mentioned above, the great biblical scholar admits that he used to invoke the Spirit of the Lord to deepen his understanding of Holy Scripture, putting his trust in the prayers of those who loved him.

In reality all true *lectio divina* from first to last is profoundly characterized by a religious attitude of prayer in all its many forms and expressions: litanies and supplications, praise and thanksgiving, confession of sin and petitions for mercy, mystical heights and contemplation. Hence, for a number of contemporary authors, *lectio divina* is defined as the "Word made prayer", that is, as a method of praying. In effect a deep listening to the Bible cannot but transform itself into prayer. The believer spontaneously feels the need to respond to the God of Love who reveals himself and speaks through Holy Scripture, with hymns, acts of thanksgiving, petitions, supplications and pleas.

The *lectio divina* then is made up of two main stages: (1) reading the Bible attentively and religiously, during which the believer *listens* to the voice of the heavenly Father who speaks very intimately; (2) the response of the faithful in *prayer*, in an attitude of adherence to the Word, of praise for the grandeur and goodness of God in the marvels of his plan of salvation. It is an attitude of petition, requesting forgiveness for shortcomings and lack of faith, and pleading for the help of God's grace. These two elements of listening and prayer are without doubt indispensable to any true "spiritual" or "existential" reading of Holy Scripture, a reading animated by the Holy Spirit and transformed into a loving dialogue. For in fact the *lectio divina* consists of a conversation between the heavenly Father and his children. On one side, God speaks through his letter, the Bible, revealing his unfathomable love for a sinful world; he reveals his ways; he admonishes his creatures. On the other side, his listening people respond and welcome the Word; they celebrate the divine goodness and wisdom; they implore God's mercy on their sinful condition; they plead for the grace to be able to respond to God's saving plan. In this way, a spiritually transformative dialogue is established through listening to the Word and the believer's prayer.

In this book we have set ourselves the goal of aiding the *lectio divina* among those faithful who do not live in monasteries. We wish to do this by showing the importance of a reading of the Bible that profoundly affects daily life, not only on an individual spiritual level but also for the apostolate and the qualitative growth of Christ's people. We follow the pattern of the Bible, offering contributions about the Old and New Testaments. In these the purpose and saving value of reading the Word come to light. The study of Holy Scripture in synagogue worship documents the love of the Jewish people for the Torah and the other inspired writings.

The *lectio divina* has left a profound imprint on the monastic spirituality of the East and West. For this reason, we have devoted a whole section to this tradition. We have benefited from the collaboration of renowned specialists, among whom we should like to pick out Jean Gribomont, who died only a few weeks after he sent in his manuscript.

The final section of this book focuses on a number of important issues that reading the Word in a way related to our life raises about the spirituality and pastoral concerns of the Church *today*. They develop some of the valuable suggestions of Vatican II in the Dogmatic Constitution on Divine Revelation. This provides the occasion for a celebrated exegete, former rector of the Pontifical Biblical Institute and of the Gregorian University of Rome, and now bishop of the largest diocese in the world, to testify to the importance of the *lectio divina* for the pastoral life of the

Church. The collection concludes with an article on the *lectio divina* as integral to the vision of the liturgy today and in the future.

Our purpose will be achieved if this book manages to offer some help to the many people who wish to practise a fruitful *lectio divina*, encouraging them to quench their thirst with the living waters of the Word, with a life-giving listening to Holy Scripture transformed into prayer.

Chapter 1

The reading of the Word in the Old Testament

Salvatore A. Panimolle

In biblical revelation an exceptionally important place is given to listening to the Word. At first sight it might appear that the reading of Scripture does not play such an important role. Indeed, the earliest tradition of both the Old and the New Testament was originally transmitted orally and only later established in writing. Even Jesus himself, the centre of revelation, simply proclaimed the Good News. He wrote neither a line nor a sentence. Only in John 8:6.8, in a passage that is textually uncertain, are we told that the prophet of Nazareth wrote in the dust.

Both the Judaic and the Christian religions, however, are shaped above all by the need to listen. The Bible frequently tells us to listen to the Lord's voice or his Word, emphasizing that the characteristic attitude of Jew or Christian in relation to God is to listen. As an instance of this, suffice it to remember the miraculous crossing of the Red Sea and Moses' call to the people following their liberation from slavery in Egypt:

> If you will diligently hearken to the voice of the Lord your God, and do that which is right in his eyes, and give heed to his commandments and keep all his statutes, I will put none of the diseases upon you which I put upon the Egyptians: for I am the Lord, your healer (Ex 15:26).

During the Exodus period the Lord continually speaks through the lips of Moses, establishes and sets his norms and his decrees (e.g., cf. Ex 19:3ff.20-23.25-31; Deut 1:16ff). Reference is only seldom made to the Torah, written by the finger of God and read by his intermediary in the assembly of Israel. The truth is that the Jews, in order to become the exclusive property of the Lord, to become a kingdom of priests and a holy nation, must listen to the voice of God and keep his covenant:

> If you will obey my voice and keep my covenant, you shall be my own possession among the peoples: for all the earth is mine, and you shall be to me a kingdom of priests and a holy nation (Ex 19:5f).

That is why Moses, before communicating the holy law to the people (summed up in the Decalogue) invites them to listen (Deut 5:1f):

> Hear, O Israel, the Lord our God is the one Lord; and you shall love the Lord your God with all your heart, and with all your soul, and with all your might (Deut 6:4f).

Moreover, the psalmist encourages the people to listen to the voice of the Lord each day:

> O that today you would hearken to his voice!
> Harden not your hearts (Ps 95:7f).

The true attitude of the just man before God, his creator and Father, is summed up by "listening". This is the purpose behind the High Priest Eli teaching the young Samuel how to respond to the voice of God calling him:

> Eli said to Samuel, "Go, lie down; and if he calls you, you shall say, 'Speak, Lord, for thy servant hears.'" So Samuel went and lay down in his place. And the Lord came and stood forth, calling as at the other times, "Samuel! Samuel!" And Samuel said, "Speak, Lord for thy servant hears" (1 Sam 3:9f).

There is a like purpose in the single command of the heavenly Father to the disciples of his Son:

> "This is my beloved Son; listen to him" (Mk 9:7).

1. The lectio divina in the Old Testament

Despite the primary role of listening and the oral transmission of divine revelation in the Bible, the reading of the

16

Word has enormous importance in the Old Testament. Indeed, it constantly grows in importance, so that Mosaic religion becomes a matter of faithfully safeguarding the Scriptures, the book of God which is read in liturgical assemblies and in private. The Bible is the Word of God preserved in paper and ink. It is the basis of the faith and the spiritual nourishment of the people of God. Therefore it must be read, interpreted and applied so as to feed all believers.

Already in the Pentateuch, although it is clear that the religion of Yahweh is founded upon the oral proclamation of the Word and the acceptance of this Word as the revealed message of God through Moses, there is evidence of the importance of reading the Decalogue and other precepts of the Lord.

These were those words written by the finger of God or by his intermediary, the great prophet of the Exodus. In fact, the ratification of the covenant between the Lord and Israel at the foot of Sinai took place during a community celebration of *lectio divina*.

a) *From the oral proclamation to the written message of Scripture*

Yahwist religion, therefore, is distinctively one of listening. Nevertheless, the Bible is a book that has taken shape gradually, gathering up the ancient oral traditions of Israel and then consigning them to paper. Indeed, the most holy and precious part was written by the finger of God. In this instance, Moses' mediation consists in *reading* the words of the Lord, written on the two stone tablets of the covenant.

In the Bible, it is possible to trace the stages of a transition from the listening to the reading of the Word. The latter stages of Scripture show that the change has already taken place. In large measure the change was the result of the lack of charismatic figures who revealed the will of God directly to his people. Moses, Joshua and the prophets normally did not read or write. They proclaimed the Word in God's name, so they were seen as the "mouth of God" (*nabîm*): indeed, they communicated the Word of Yahweh. Moses' vocation is both illustrative and instructive: his mission in life is to lend his voice to the Lord who will speak in him:

> Moses said to the Lord, "Oh, my Lord, I am not eloquent, either heretofore or since thou hast spoken to thy servant; but I am slow of speech and of tongue." Then the Lord said to him, "Who has made man's mouth? Who makes him dumb, or seeing, or blind? Is it not I, the Lord? Now therefore, go, and I will be with your mouth and teach you what you shall speak." But he said, "Oh, my Lord, send, I pray, some other person." Then the anger of the Lord was kindled against Moses and he said, "Is there not Aaron, your brother, the Levite? I know he can speak well; and behold, he is coming out to meet you and when he sees you, he will be glad in his heart. And you shall speak to him and put the words in his mouth; and I will be with your mouth and with his mouth, and will teach you what you shall do. He shall speak for you to the people; and he shall be a mouth for you, and you shall be to him as God" (Ex 4:10-16).

On a number of occasions the Prophets are commanded to put their oracles in writing. In Isaiah it is plain that the oracle is to be cut out clearly on a table that might serve as an everlasting witness:

> And now, go, write it before them on a tablet,
> and inscribe it in a book,
> that it may be for the time to come
> as a witness for ever (Is 30:8).

The prophecies of Jeremiah were also written down either in a book or on scrolls (cf. Jer 25:13; 30:2; 51:60). The Lord commanded the prophet to write all that had been revealed to him on a scroll (Jer 36:4ff.18.27.32; 45:1). And the prophet Habakkuk receives a similar command from the Lord:

> Write the vision;
> make it plain upon tablets,
> so he may run who reads it (Hab 2:2).

All the same, the main activity of the prophets was to proclaim the Word of God, not to read it. It is only towards the end of the Davidic monarchy that we encounter the drawing together of the ancient traditions of the Pentateuch, which were placed on parchment scrolls and locked securely in the Temple at Jerusalem. The description of when they were rediscovered in the Temple at the time of King Josiah (2 Kings 22:3) illustrates this literary phenomenon. This process matured and was consolidated during the exile in Babylon. On the restoration of the Jewish state in the time of Ezra and Nehemiah, this process seems to be coming to a conclusion. At this time the people of God refer to the Law as written in ink, on the pages of a book or parchment rolls, and thus called "Scripture". The Law comes to be read and studied by scribes, the teachers of the Bible, so that it can then be proclaimed and explained in the assemblies of Israel. The point in Israel's history has been reached when the age of the prophets has passed away and the age of the "Book" begins. The Bible is the great treasure of Israel. It is guarded carefully, studied in depth, and put into practice particularly by men consecrated to the "Book". This, then, is how the *lectio divina* is carried out.

In point of fact, the first record of the Word being read in the Bible goes back to the origins of the Mosaic religion during the exodus, on the occasion of one of the most solemn and important events in the life of Israel, the event that can be seen as the birth of the people of God: the conclusion of the covenant at the foot of Sinai (Ex 24:3-8). Here we find the most ancient witness of the *lectio divina*, which takes place in a liturgical setting.

Exodus 24:4 tells us of the beginning of the shift from oral proclamation to the putting down of the Word of God in writing. For Moses does not only communicate the prophecies and the precepts of the Lord; he carefully writes them down. It is true that he had already been commanded to write down in a book all that had happened against the Amalekites (Ex 17:14). The same command is repeated concerning the conditions of the covenant (Ex 34:10-26):

> Write these words; in accordance with these words I have made a covenant with you and with Israel (Ex 34:27).

The Torah is thus considered to be written by Moses (cf.

19

Deut 31:9). In other texts on the book of Exodus, however, there is the tradition that God in person wrote the Decalogue on the two tablets of stone:

> The Lord said to Moses, "Come up to me on the mountain, and wait there; and I will give you the tables of stone, with the law and the commandment, which I have written for their instruction" (Ex 24:12). The Lord said to Moses, "Cut two tables of stone like the first; and I will write upon the tables the words that were on the first tables, which you broke" (Ex 34:1).

Exodus 34:28f tells us that the Lord wrote the ten words of the covenant on the two tablets of the testimony, while Moses was on Mount Sinai, in order that they be read in the solemn assembly of the people of Israel. The tablets of the testimony are described as tablets written by the finger of God (cf. Ex 31:18; Deut 4:13; 9:10), hence they are the work of God and the writing of God:

> And Moses turned, and went down the mountain with the two tables of the testimony in his hands, tables that were written on both sides; on the one side and on the other were they written. And the tables were the work of God, graven upon the tables (Ex 32:15f).

The book of Deuteronomy made it plain that the two tablets written by the Lord were kept in the ark of the covenant:

> At that time the Lord said to me, "Hew two tables of stone like the first, and come up the mountain, and make an ark of wood. And I will write on the tables the words that were on the first tables you broke, and you shall put them in the ark." So I made an ark of acacia wood, and hewed two tables of stone like the first and went up the mountain with the two tables in my hand. And he wrote on the tables, as at the first writing, the ten commandments which the Lord had spoken to you on the mountain out of the midst of the fire on the day of the assembly; and the Lord gave them to me. Then I turned and came from the mountain, and put the tables in the ark which I had made; and there they are as the Lord commanded me (Deut 10:1-5).

By the time of this last book of the Pentateuch, the process of consigning the Torah to writing seems to have been completed (cf. Deut 28:58.61; 29:19f; 30:10). When he had finished writing the book of the Law, Moses entrusted it to the Levites, commanding them to put it next to the ark of the covenant, so that it might be a witness against all of Israel's rebellions:

> When Moses had finished writing the words of this law in a book, to the very end, Moses commanded the Levites who carried the ark of the covenant of the Lord, "Take this book of the law, and put it by the side of the ark of the covenant of the Lord your God, that it may be there for a witness against you. For I know how rebellious and stubborn you are" (Deut 31:24-27).

For this reason, the king of Israel always had to have a copy of the Torah for his own personal use, so as to meditate upon it every day:

> And when he sits on the throne of his kingdom, he shall write for himself in a book a copy of this law, from that which is in the charge of the Levitical priests; and it shall be with him, and he shall read it all the days of his life, that he may learn to fear the Lord his God, by keeping all the words of this law and these statutes, and doing them (Deut 17:18f).

All the people, indeed, must write the words of the Torah on tall stones coated with lime (Deut 27:1-3.8). And Joshua, after the entry of Israel into Palestine, wrote a copy of the Law of Moses on stones (Josh 8:32), adding, indeed, the statutes and ordinances given at Shechem (Josh 24:25f).

b) *Listening to the Word when read*

Revelation was written to be read: in private but above all in the liturgical assembly of the whole people of God. That is why the Israelites, including those who could not read, listened to the reading out of the Lord's words written in the Torah. Scripture was proclaimed with great solemnity. The most important members of the community read the Word of God before the whole assembly, for instance, Moses (Ex 24:7), Joshua his successor (Josh 8:34), Ezra the priest (Neh 8:3) and the most distinguished Levites (Neh 8:7f). In these assemblies, the reader had to stand in a raised position in order to be heard clearly. In Nehemiah 8:3 it is said specifically that Ezra fulfilled that office from a wooden platform, a kind of primitive pulpit.

In this way, though to some extent mutedly, the importance of listening to the Word is suggested once again. In this case it was not a matter of hearing a spoken prophetic utterance or an oral tradition that had been learnt by heart. It was a written page, read with solemnity, that was proclaimed to the people. Thus the primacy of listening in the Bible can be seen again.

In truth the conversion of the heart comes through hearing the Word proclaimed by the reader. This much is clear from the examples already given. Similarly in private reading it is necessary to hear, though inwardly.

It is a question of the Word penetrating through the eyes or the ears to the heart. Consequently in the early centuries, in the monasteries the normal practice of private *lectio divina* was to read aloud: what was read was proclaimed, even alone in one's cell.

2. *Models of* lectio divina *in the Old Testament*

We have seen how reading and proclaiming Scripture goes back to the origins of the Mosaic religion. In the following pages we would like to look in more depth at the passages of Scripture that are most significant for this subject. They give an instructive example of how we ought to carry out our own *lectio divina*. These pericopes contain a rich and stimulating teaching with regard to a profound and attentive hearing of the Word.

a) *The* lectio divina *at the foot of Mount Sinai*

As noted above, Exodus 24:3-8 provides us with one of the most ancient descriptions of reading the Word of God. It describes a true *lectio divina* that takes place in a liturgical assembly. It marks the conclusion of the covenant between the Lord and Israel, the act that brings to birth the people of God.

Scholars maintain that this passage is part of the Elohist tradition in the Pentateuch and, as a passage, it seems to form a whole. Indeed, we can clearly see a thematic inclusion, expressed by the term *"all the words of the Lord"* at the beginning (Ex 24:3) and in the end by the expression "the covenant which the Lord has made with you in accordance with *all these words"* (Ex 28:8).

As described here the liturgy has two main elements: the reading of the Law and the sprinkling of the blood of sacrificed animals. Both were necessary to conclude the covenant between the Lord and his people, because ancient Semitic ceremonial validated pacts by sacrificing animals, the blood of which was sprinkled over both parties once the terms of the agreement had been announced.

In this instance, we want to highlight the element of the reading of the Word. As the passage opens, we are told that Moses had written all the words of the Lord (Ex 24:4) revealed to him on Mount Sinai (Ex 24:1f). What is meant here is the book of the covenant which contained the Ten Commandments above all. And Moses read it out before the whole of the people (Ex 24:7). Before the pact with the Lord could be concluded, Israel had to know the norms and the conditions laid down by its God. Therefore, the mediator of the covenant had to proclaim the laws contained in the book of the covenant. It was a solemn and important reading, because without it the Hebrew people would not know the terms of its pact with the Lord. As a result the Israelites knew that the Lord was and would forever remain their one and only God. That is why idolatry is severely forbidden; indeed, it becomes an abomination in the sight of the Lord, who is a jealous God. The Israelites would have to worship and serve the Lord alone, and furthermore, they would have to be careful not to take his name in vain as well as pay attention to observe his commandments (cf. Ex 20:1f).

Then the assembly of Israel replied to the reading of the

terms of the covenant, committing itself to doing all that its God demanded:

All that the Lord has spoken we will do, and we will be obedient (Ex 24:7).

The purpose of the proclaiming of the Word has been achieved: it has brought about a positive response in all the people.

These, then, are the essential elements in the liturgical *lectio divina*: the solemn proclamation of the Word which leads to acceptance by its hearers! At Sinai Moses began the practice of reading God's book. It was to form the central nucleus of Hebrew and Christian liturgy, indeed to be the vital nourishment of believers. They feed upon the words that come from the mouth of the Lord by carefully and lovingly reading Scripture.

b) *The* lectio divina *and the whole people of Israel*

The historical books of the Old Testament record that the solemn reading of Scripture before the whole people did not take place only at the foot of Sinai, when the covenant was made. The most important examples of these other occasions can be found in Joshua 8:32-35; 2 Kings 23:1-3; Nehemiah 8:1-12. Furthermore in Deuteronomy 31:9-13, Moses is commanded to read the whole Torah before all of Israel every seven years.

Joshua 8:30-35 describes a liturgy similar to that of Exodus 24:4-8. It is composed of two elements: a rite of sacrifice on a stone altar and the reading of the Word of God. But while in Exodus 24:4 the emphasis is placed upon the rites of sacrifice and the sprinkling of blood upon the altar and the Israelites, in Joshua 8:30ff the emphasis is placed upon the reading of the law of Moses.

It is in this last passage that we are told that Joshua copied the law of Moses onto stones (Josh 8:32), following in the footsteps of the great Exodus hero (Ex 24:4). In Joshua 8:33, however, the attitude of those participating in the liturgy of the reading of Scripture is described:

> And all Israel, sojourner as well as homeborn, with their elders and officers and their judges, stood on opposite sides of the ark before the Levitical priests who carried the ark of the covenant of the Lord, half of them in front of Mount Gerizim and half of them in front of Mount Ebal.

The assembly includes women, children and strangers living in the midst of the Israelites (Josh 8:35), and the liturgical high point is the diligent proclamation of the whole of the Torah:

> And afterwards he read all the words of the law, the blessing and the curse, according to all that is written in the book of the law. There was not a word of all that Moses commanded which Joshua did not read before all the assembly of Israel (Josh 8:34f).

With this reading of the blessing and curse contained in the Torah to the whole of the people in two groups, one facing Mount Gerizim and the other facing Mount Ebal (Josh 8:33ff), Joshua fulfils the Mosaic command recorded in the last book of the Pentateuch (Deut 11:29; 27:11ff). The Word is read before the most precious and holy object of Israel: the ark of the covenant. It is in the centre of the assembly, the participants standing "on opposite sides of the ark before the Levitical priests who carried the ark of the covenant of the Lord" (Josh 8:33). This casket of wood, covered with gold-leaf (Ex 37:1), housed the tablets of stone on which the Ten Commandments were inscribed (Ex 24:12; 25:16; 40:20; 1 Kings 8:9.) Hence it was called the ark of the testimony (Ex 25:22; 26:33ff; 40:3.5.21). This liturgy of the Word takes place in the open, in the sight of the Lord, of whose presence the ark is the visible sign. Indeed, the ark is a holy object that only the Levitical priests can touch, while other Israelites may not on pain of death (cf. Josh 3:3f; 2 Sam 6:1-11).

In the last book of the Pentateuch, however, it is envisaged that the solemn reading of the Torah is to be done in the holy place that the Lord would choose for the dwelling of his glory (Deut 31:9ff), namely, the Temple of Jerusalem, where the Lord will establish his name, or in other words, his presence (Deut 12:4-12; 1 Kings 6:12f; 8:1-13).

In Deuteronomy 31:9-13 is written what Moses ordained concerning the reading of the Torah to the whole people:

> At the end of every seven years, at the set time of release, at the season of the booths, when all Israel comes to appear before the Lord your God at the place which he shall choose, you shall read this law before all Israel in their hearing. Assemble the people, men, women and little ones, and the sojourner within your towns, that they may hear and learn to fear the Lord your God, and be careful to do all the words of this law (Deut 31:10-13).

As a result of this ordinance, a liturgy of the Word was to be celebrated every seventh year in the Temple in Jerusalem. This was in the jubilee year and during the Feast of the Tabernacles, which was held in the autumn and lasted a week (cf. Deut 16:13ff; Lev 23:34ff). The whole people had to go up to the Temple and listen to the Law being proclaimed by the priests, sons of Levi, and by the elders of the people (Deut 31:9ff).

During this ceremony, participated in not only by men and women but also children and foreigners living in Hebrew cities, the teachers of Israel read the Torah to everyone, so that they could all hear the Word, learn to fear the Lord, and commit themselves to following the Law's demands. In this way, even those Israelites who ignored the Law learnt to fear the Lord by hearing his words (Deut 31:12f).

The point of this *lectio divina* was to arouse the fear of Yahweh: "that they may... learn to fear the Lord your God" (Deut 31:12.13). Obviously this is a reverent fear of going against the Lord's precepts, of not living up to the terms of the covenant. It is fear that is the fruit of love, as suggested in particular by Deuteronomy 10:12f and 13:2-5. In these verses the fear of God is shown as meaning the same thing as love or the expression of Israel's consecration of its whole being to the Lord.

2 Kings 22:3-12 contains an important and interesting model for the *lectio divina*. It is when the Torah is redis-

covered in the Temple and then read by the scribe Shaphan, first of all privately before King Josiah, and then publicly before the people in the Temple of Jerusalem. It has signs of both the personal and the solemn, liturgical kinds of *lectio divina*. The scene is important because of the healthy effects that the reading has: it was the beginning of the religious reform in the kingdom of Judah.

When King Josiah heard the words of the Torah read by Shaphan, he was deeply disturbed and wept, prostrating himself before the Lord, and he tore his garments in sorrow and fear of the divine punishment for being so ignorant of the commandments of the Law (2 Kings 22:8-13.19). The proclamation of the Word had a good effect in the King's heart and began a profound conversion of all the people of Judah.

Indeed, Josiah called together a general assembly of all the men of Judah and the inhabitants of Jerusalem, all the people, great and small, for a solemn liturgy of the Word. The book of the covenant found in the Temple was read in their presence (2 Kings 23:1f). This liturgical celebration led to the covenant concluded by the King

> before the Lord, to walk after the Lord and to keep his commandments and his testimonies and his statutes, with all his heart and all his soul, to perform the words of this covenant that were written in this book; and all the people joined the covenant (2 Kings 23:3).

Hence the liturgical *lectio divina* brought about the solemn renewal of the pact with the Lord. As a result, the idols are removed from the Temple, the idolatrous priests are deposed, the houses of the cult prostitutes are demolished (2 Kings 23:4ff). Reading the Word produced excellent effects, with a conversion of heart on the part of Josiah and of the Israelites, and leading to the profound renewal of the people of God.

c) *The* lectio divina *of the King of Israel*

Josiah's religious reform described above came about because of the rediscovery and the reading of the Torah. The kings of Israel were charged with ensuring the observance of the law of the Lord.

The religious condition of Israel depended in large measure upon the faith and commitment of its monarchs. That is why the author of Deuteronomy lays down that when the King is enthroned, he must write

> for himself a copy of this law, from that which is in charge of the Levitical priests; and it shall be with him, and he shall read in it all the days of his life, that he may learn to fear the Lord his God, by keeping all the words of this law and these statutes (Deut 17:18f).

The King of Israel, then, must observe a daily *lectio divina*, to become familiar with the Word of the Lord and make it more and more his own. In this way, the Word becomes the spiritual nourishment of his life and the standard by which he acts and governs.

d) *The* lectio divina *as described in Jeremiah 36:1-32*

Unfortunately the reading of the Word did not always effect conversions, nor were people always willing to listen to the voice of the Lord speaking through the writings of his servants. There is a vivid description of King Jehoiakim's stubbornness in the book of Jeremiah. The King did not want to accept the prophet's message. In fact, he cut up the scroll upon which the prophetic pronouncements were written and tossed it into the fire. He even wanted to throw the prophet himself into prison (Jer 36:21ff). Before this dramatic event takes place, some interesting scenes are described which concern the reading of the Word of God.

Jeremiah is commanded by the Lord to write down on a scroll all the divine prophecies from the days of King Josiah. They are to be read out to the house of Judah in order to invite conversion and so obtain God's pardon (Jer 36:1ff). Baruch, on having written down the prophetic messages that were dictated to him, went to the Temple to proclaim the Lord's words. This was following Jeremiah's command:

> You are to go, and on a fast day in the hearing of all the people in the Lord's house you shall read the words of the Lord from the scroll which you have written at my dictation. You shall read them also in the hearing of all the men of Judah who come out of their cities. It may be that their supplication will come before the Lord, and that every one will turn from his evil way (Jer 36:6f).

Two points about Jeremiah's injunction are striking:

(i) *the way of proclamation:* the reading had to be done in a loud voice, so that everyone in the Temple could hear it; (ii) *the purpose* of this *lectio divina*: it was to effect conversion and give rise to the desire to implore the Lord's mercy, that he might turn aside his anger and wrath from his people.

Then, after Micaiah, Shaphan's grandson, had told the leaders of Judah what had been said in the Temple, Baruch repeats the prophecies of Jeremiah before them. When they hear the prophecies, the leaders feel shaken and afraid, and they decide to inform the King (Jer 36:16-20).

This passage is especially interesting because of the effect that the reading of the Word has upon its hearers. Although the way in which the common people responded to the message is not recorded, there are opposing reactions from the leaders and the King. The leaders are deeply impressed; however, when they inform the monarch, not only is he unmoved, but he destroys the scroll bearing the Word of the Lord, even going so far as to wish to imprison the mediators of the divine message.

Such obstinacy of heart seals the fate of the King and accelerates his disastrous downfall. Rejection of the Word spells not only spiritual but temporal ruin. Soon Jehoiakim loses his grip on the government of Judah and comes to an ignominious end: he is killed and left without burial (Jer 36:29f).

Some similar fate might yet be the lot of all those who refuse to listen to the voice of the Lord in the Scriptures, preferring to follow their own ways; thus making themselves inaccessible to the Word which wants only to save, to give fulness of life and joy.

Chapter 2

Bible reading in the Jewish tradition

Riccardo Di Segni

One cannot begin to speak about the liturgical practice of reading the Bible without first of all defining the concepts and structures concerning ritual. These are the context in which the liturgy is located, completing and perfecting them as an organic whole. To omit doing so would distort the perspective, making any analysis incomplete, particularly as such information is necessary for a comparative study or a search for historical "roots".

1. *Studying the Bible as a basic religious obligation*

In the Jewish tradition there has always been an emphasis upon the constant and continual relationship between the believer and the biblical text. The Bible contains all the principles of the Jewish faith, though not in a purely formal way, as a polite recognition that remains an end in itself. Rather the relationship is of an indissoluble bond, the very ground of one's existence, for it "means life to you and length of days" (Deut 30:20). Consequently, as God commanded Joshua at the beginning of his ministry: "This book of the law shall not depart out of your mouth, but you shall meditate [*wehaghita*] on it day and night" (Josh 1:8).

The traditional Jewish name for the Pentateuch is Torah; it means "teaching". It is the guide to life and life's very fountain. The Torah is the expression of God's eternal love for his people Israel. In the opinion of Rabbi Shimon bar Yochai it is one of the three wonderful gifts that God has given Israel, together with the land of Israel and the world to

31

come. None of the three is granted automatically, but each must be sustained with effort and suffering (TB *Ber.* 5a).

Every Jew is called to reciprocate that divine love with the constant struggle to love the Lord his God: "You shall love the Lord your God with all your heart, and with all your soul, and with all your might" (Deut 6:5). How then is this commitment expressed? According to the biblical teaching that follows upon this basic principle, the believer's relationship of love concentrates on two things: praxis and study. Both are necessary and indivisible. One must never be favoured to the detriment of the other.

Keeping in mind and having an inner knowledge of "these words" is the light that guides and gives full meaning to righteous behaviour:

> And these words which I command you this day shall be upon your heart; and you shall teach them diligently to your children, and shall talk of them when you sit in your house, and when you walk by the way, and when you lie down, and when you rise (Deut 6:6-7).

Praxis in itself is not sufficient. There is also the need to make the effort to understand and to study, to set aside a regular time each day in the morning and at night. One should not lose an opportunity to study lest it never recur (*Avot* 2:4).

In the rabbinical world the study of the Torah is regarded as an integral element of religious life. It is of equal value to all the other norms of religious practice. For this study is the key to understanding, and the cultural expression, of a system based on practical observance. It is difficult to find any other religious system which accords a higher place to study than Judaism, precisely as a way of showing a faithful love for the Creator.

This religious duty embraces everyone; no one can abstain from studying; it can be neither reserved nor delegated to some elite band. It is a norm that has enormous religious and social implications. It changes the way in which society and class structure are ordered, for culture in Judaism is a method for social advancement. Ignorance is considered as without merit or justification; the ignorant are not pious nor has the uncouth any fear of sin (*Avot* 2:5). In rabbinic thought culture outweighs nobility of birth: "It is better to be a wise bastard than an ignorant chief priest" (*Horayot* 13b).

From this perspective, inspired by Deuteronomy, one sees the further duty to transmit one's knowledge to all future generations. Parents must teach their children. No occasion should be missed. Nor is anyone exempt from this obligation; it cannot be delegated to any other group or caste. It is a family obligation both to transmit the knowledge and provide a model of life. There is no room for, "when they grow up they can choose for themselves". Judaism recognizes that everyone has the intellectual capacity to choose for him or herself at any moment in life, but it is also clear that there is a duty to point out the possibility of choice and to show that on one side there is goodness and life (Deut 30:19). Silence and omission, in the Jewish mind, are not regarded as signs of liberalism, but rather the passive acceptance of models of living from alien cultures, which willingly or unwillingly the world has succeeded in transmitting.

Study and teaching then require individual Jews, families and institutions to organize their time and their way of life. There can be no community without a teacher or a school. For at least twenty centuries among the Jews instruction was not only obligatory but also free of charge. There is merit in the one who studies; there is merit and honour in the one who teaches.

2. Every individual should write his own copy of the Torah

Relationship with Scripture is expressed in a variety of liturgical practices and forms. One in particular deserves close attention since it is often overlooked. It concerns the obligation of each Jew not only to read but also to write for himself a copy of the Pentateuch. This is not just any old

33

copy; rather it is a document written in accordance with detailed and precise regulations. It is copied on specially-prepared parchment taken from an approved animal. The ink, which is black, is made up following a particular recipe and has a special consistency so that it stands out strikingly and lasts for a long time. The pen must not be made of metal since from metal come weapons, the instruments of death. The writer must cleanse himself in mind and body, above all when it comes to copying the letters of the divine names.

The master text must be rigorously respected; no copy is valid which contains the slightest error. When Jesus spoke of the "jot and the tittle" it was to this he was referring. The copy thus prepared becomes something sacred. The scroll of the Pentateuch, the *Sefer Torah*, must be honoured and protected. Hence it is customarily stored in a special cupboard on the east side of the Synagogue. It is decked with embroidered cloth studded with precious stones.

Everyone is obliged to make his own book. Those not in a position to do so personally, because they are unable to read or write, have to commission an expert to do it for them. The scriptural grounds on which the rabbis justify this are rather weak. They are based on a verse which says: "Now therefore write this song, and teach it to the people of Israel" (Deut 31:19). The canticle referred to can be found in chapter 32. The logic is as follows. Merely writing the canticle itself is not sufficient to respect the integrity of the whole text. Therefore everyone must write out the full text. Apart from this particular consideration, the rabbinic injunction displays an exceptional concern for the written text, both its transmission and its study. The copying of the text word for word is of major consequence; attention to the smallest detail presumes a care and deep affection for that which one is copying far and above the concentration given to any old text which must merely be read. It means imposing a respect for every particular, putting under scrutiny the smallest detail because in each one lies a hidden truth and a teaching. Even when an ordinary person has to delegate the task to someone else, the cost of procuring the copy is an incentive to check and respect that for which one has had to make a sacrifice. It is human nature to take great care of those things which cost a great deal, as opposed to things gained for free. Again this rabbinical rule shows the desire to ensure the maximum knowledge and diffusion of the text which everyone without exception must possess.

In the Jewish culture there seem never to have been any restrictions or censorship when studying the Bible (except in very special cases such as the public study of Ezekiel 1; cf. *Mishnah Hagierah* 2:1). Not only *can* everyone, but everyone *must* go to the texts, and each person should own his own copy. Freedom of interpretation is a necessary corollary of this attitude. The rabbis distinguish between the observance of the Law and everything else. No one is exempt from practising the Law; its norms must be followed just as they are. Dissent from this model of behaviour is not permissible.

However, outside of this, in every other matter, from styles of textual criticism to critical interpretation, dissent is welcomed because it stimulates discussion. It is typical of rabbinical texts to have different opinions on the same subject put forward at the same time. Each word becomes "a Word of the living God", even that of two differently opposed schools of thought. Truth lies in discussion, not in dogma.

3. *Liturgical forms of reading the Bible*

After this obligation to study and write out the Pentateuch, the rabbinical tradition lays down liturgical times to read the Scriptures, and gives precise details as to how this should be done.

This would appear to be an ancient custom and probably comes from when the canon of the text was defined. It is difficult to pinpoint precisely the period when the rituals were established. Within the rabbinical tradition, it is a matter about which opinions vary and the views of critics likewise vary. The most generally accepted opinion dates the public reading of extracts from the Pentateuch at set times in the week, from the time of Ezra, namely, to the period of the return from Babylonian captivity.

The more traditional rabbis would date the practice further back to the time of Moses, leaving to Ezra only minor details of arrangement. In either event the Torah has been read at fixed times since the days of Ezra. With the establishment of the Synagogue this custom assumed a more and more precise liturgical form. Normally the reading takes place on all feast days, starting with the Sabbath, in the course of the morning service. On the Sabbath there is also a short reading and an afternoon prayer added. So that the readings be not too far separated from each other, two weekday readings were fitted in, on Mondays and Thursdays. It seems that both these days were chosen because in ancient times they were market days and therefore there was the likelihood of more people being present.

Nowadays the whole Pentateuch is read over the year. The text is divided up into passages (*parashiyat*) for every Sabbath throughout the year. This manner of selection is now common everywhere, but for at least a millennium there existed side by side with it another custom, peculiar to the Palestinian Jews and diaspora communities closely connected with them, such as the Italian Jews.

According to their tradition the Pentateuch is read over a period of three and a half years. This means that the Torah is read twice every seven years, the sabbatical cycle. At present this cycle begins and ends in autumn on the feast of the first month. The occasion is celebrated with a festival called *Simchat Torah*, literally, the Joy of the Torah. The highpoint comes when two members of the community are honoured by being entrusted with the changeover of the readings, one ending the other beginning. They are known as the "husbands" respectively of the Torah and of *Bereshit*, the Pentateuch and the Book of Genesis.

Reading the Torah in the Synagogue is only permissible when ten adults are present. Ten is the necessary quorum for all important liturgical functions (for without this minimal nucleus of the community one would lose the particular solemnity of the reading). The liturgical reading begins with the solemn withdrawal of the parchment scroll from the cupboard in which it has been stored. The scroll is carried in procession to the table and is placed there to be read. Its decorative coverings are removed and it is raised up on high for all to see (at the beginning or at the end of the reading according to different customs). The biblical text to be read is divided into several parts (from three to seven, depending on the solemnity of the feast). Each part is deputed to a member of the community who is called to read by the superintendent. The reader recites a prayer of blessing and then, where it is possible, reads directly from the Hebrew text; where this cannot be done then a cantor is delegated to do so. The reading must be performed with the utmost precision in pronunciation, correct diction and respect; any mistake means the word or the verse is repeated. The text is intoned in line with the tones (te'amin, neums) from the masoretic tradition. This is an extremely old tradition that has various forms (to the point where practically every community has its own particular style of intonation). These are being studied closely today in the hope of identifying common liturgical roots with the most ancient Christian liturgical traditions.

On completion of the reading, the designated reader concludes with a final prayer of blessing. There are strict rules of procedure as to who might read in the assembly. It is customary for first choice to go to the Cohenim, that is, the descendants of the priestly families; their surname reminds us of their family origins. After them it is the turn of the Levites, the members of Moses' tribe; they carry the surname Levi. Finally, any other member of the community.

When the Pentateuch reading is over, on Sabbaths and particular feastdays, a reading from the prophets is added (*haftarah*). The content of the text is related to the previous reading or, on feast days, highlights an aspect of the feast. This custom seems to have been introduced at a time when the Jews were forbidden to read the Torah. The prophetical text was read as a way of circumventing this prohibition but the content was always in line with the Torah reading. When the time of persecution ended the custom carried on. The texts read now are solidly traditional, though they vary from community to community. In the past, probably, there was a wide measure of freedom. It is most likely that Luke 4:16 refers to Jesus being called to the reading of the *haftarah*. It is customary also to invite someone who can intone the *haftarah* whose melody is different from that of the Torah. In many places there is the practice of reserving the reading to young people so that very quickly they become educated by and familiar with the text.

When the prophetical reading is completed the rabbi blesses the community recalling all the worthy people and the martyrs of the past. The scroll of the Torah is then replaced in its place of safety.

A custom that began at the time of the Babylonian captivity is now no longer in use. It had led to the spread of the Aramaic language, a side effect of which was to weaken the knowledge of Hebrew. To safeguard against this, the rabbis ruled that simultaneous Aramaic translation of the original Hebrew text should accompany the reading of the Hebrew version. *Targum* is the name of this translation. The *Turgeman* was the person who did the translating. Today the text read is Hebrew; the Aramaic is never read publicly. It would be even more unintelligible than the original Hebrew. Nowadays with bilingual texts on opposite pages of the book it is relatively easy to follow the original Hebrew text being read in public. The Targum, however, in various modes continues to be edited and published for study. It provides a most ancient key to understanding and reading the original text.

A further practice alongside the liturgical reading of the biblical text, dating from rabbinical times, is the *derashah* or the rabbinical dissertation on the text rendered in the assembly. The rabbi or someone else of similar cultural standing addresses the community, commenting on the biblical text with a view to deepening understanding. Formerly the *derashah* followed a fixed pattern of procedures differing from community to community. From this point of view the tradition is growing weaker, though the homily still retains its essential importance. Indeed, it is in the homily that the relationship between teacher and community, and community and written tradition is most concretely expressed. For in the homily is the most obvious demonstration of the constant effort and challenge to enter into dialogue with the cultural basis of Jewish tradition, the uninterrupted source of instruction and life.

Chapter 3

Reading the Word
in the New Testament

Salvatore A. Panimolle

The New Testament takes the practice of *lectio divina* for granted; it refers to it at times and describes moments when the Word is proclaimed, commented upon and inspires action. Naturally, like the writers of the Old Testament, the New Testament writers attach more importance to listening to the Word than to reading it.

We find no divine command to read the Bible but on the contrary we are told of the Father's injunction to listen to his beloved Son (Mk 9:9). Furthermore, Jesus invites people to listen to his teaching (cf. Mk 4:5.9.23; 7:14.16 and parallel verses). James follows in this tradition calling on his people to love listening to the Word (Jas 1:9). Throughout the New Testament there is an emphasis on the primacy of listening to the Word.

This being granted, it is important to recognize that reading the Scriptures is not totally ignored in the New Testament; indeed it is a central New Testament theme.

Paul of Tarsus insists upon it. He fully intended his letters to be read by all the brethren in those communities to which they had been sent (1 Tit 5:27; Col 4:16; Eph 3:4). He expects them to be passed around to other Churches (Col 4:16). He refers explicitly to reading the Torah as it was practised in the synagogues, stressing how difficult it is to transform this exercise into a true *lectio divina* (2 Cor 3:12ff).

In the synoptics too we find a number of interesting allusions to reading the Word of God by the Jewish people.

41

The Prophet of Nazareth appeals to the current practice to further his own teaching.

1. *The Jewish practice of reading the Word*

There are a number of New Testament references to Bible reading in the time of Jesus and Paul. The Prophet of Nazareth refers more than once to reading the Old Testament when confronting his adversaries; it is taken for granted as something very normal.

a) *Biblical evidence for reading the Word*

Jesus frequently assumes reading the Torah as the starting point for his own teaching, particularly in his disputes with the leaders of the people and the rabbis. Reference to Scripture forms an important element in his Galilean and Judaean ministry.

(i) *Reading the Bible as a whole.* In the controversy over the Sabbath rest caused by the disciples' violation of the Sabbath precept, Jesus, before propounding his own revolutionary teaching on the authentic finality of the festive rest and the lordship of the Son of Man over the Sabbath (Mk 2:27f), illustrates with a biblical example the hierarchy in God's commandments by citing the example of David and his companions eating the sacred loaves, reserved solely for the priests (Mk 2:25f). Here Jesus defends himself against the Jews by pointing to the custom of reading from the Bible: "Have you never read what David did, when he was in need and was hungry, he and those who were with him?" The tactic seems to have been convincing because Jesus was addressing people who were familiar with the Scriptures. It was the principal religious duty of all pious Jews to read and meditate upon the Word of God. One could certainly number the Pharisees, with whom Jesus was arguing, among these.

The passage not only has Christological implications, because Jesus proclaims his lordship of the Sabbath, but also ethical implications, because it highlights the true purpose of the Sabbath. At the same time, it says something of the *lectio divina,* for Jesus shows that reading the Bible as a whole helps in the formation of an upright conscience, a conscience formed and enlightened by the Word of God.

Indeed, it is only when texts are taken out of context and then inflated out of proportion, without bearing in mind the overall message of Scripture, that errors in interpretation occur. The Sabbath precept is a case in point. An accurate reading of the whole of the word of God points to the meaning of particular passages, keeping them all in correct proportion. That is why there is no substitute for a regular and careful reading of the whole Bible, in order to see things in their entirety and so discover the deep purpose of the divine author.

This same point is again manifest in that first dispute of Jesus' Galilean ministry concerning the indissolubility of marriage (Mk 10:2). The Mosaic Law of Deuteronomy (24:1) taken as it stands, seems clear: divorce is permissible. Jesus, on the other hand, invites us to situate the meaning of marriage within its particular original perspective given by the Creator, as described at the beginning of Genesis (1:27; 2:24). In this regard only Matthew refers explicitly to reading the Scripture, though Mark does so implicitly. Jesus answers the Pharisees' question with one of his own: "Have you not read that he who made them from the beginning made them male and female?" (Mt 19:4). In other words Jesus is saying that it is clear from reading the first chapters of the Torah that permission for divorce is not in harmony with the original purpose of marriage as conceived by the Creator; it should be monogamous and indissoluble. When one meditates upon the condition of our first parents as described in Genesis, the divorcist regime of Deuteronomy stands out in sharp contrast. The Prophet of Nazareth comments on "the two shall be one flesh" saying: "So they are no longer two but one. What therefore God has joined together, let no man put asunder" (Mk 10:8f).

Such a trenchant criticism of the existing Mosaic Law is only possible from someone steeped in the Scriptures as a whole. Only when the Bible is read sensitively under the guidance of the Holy Spirit, is it possible for people to emerge imbued with the Word, capable of discerning the mutable from the immutable elements of the biblical message, able to distinguish what is relative – and hence expendable – from what is absolute and original within divine revelation.

(ii) *Reading the Word and penetrating its meaning.* In the argument with the Sadducees over the resurrection from the dead (Mk 12:18ff), Jesus bases his final argument on what can be read in the book of Moses. To those astute adversaries who concocted the funny story of the woman married legally to seven brothers (vv. 20ff), Jesus addresses the following rhetorical question: "And as for the dead being raised, have you not read in the book of Moses..." (v. 26).

The clear teaching of Scripture is that God is not God of the dead, but of the living (v. 27). A profound reading of the Bible, therefore, grasps also the truth of the final destiny of man. At the theophany in Exodus, God reveals himself as the God of the Patriarchs. Meditating on this, it is only logical to conclude that if he is the God of the living then Abraham, Isaac and Jacob must be living after their death. So important then is it to listen attentively to the Word of God, to read and meditate upon it, in order to understand the richness of its teaching.

(iii) *Reading the Old Testament from a Christological viewpoint.* In two extracts from the synoptic gospels, what is read in the Bible is seen from the viewpoint of its fulfilment: all that Scripture contains is brought to completion in the life of Jesus. This can be seen in the children's welcome of the Son of David into Jerusalem (Mt 21:5f) and in the exaltation of the Son who would be rejected and put to death by the Jewish leaders (Mk 12:6-11 and parallel texts). At the moment of messianic entry into Jerusalem the Prophet of Nazareth was greeted in triumph, and then in the Temple the children pick up the adults' acclamation and cry out: "Hosanna to the Son of David!" (Mt 21:5).

The chief priests are scandalized when they hear this. They express their consternation to Jesus who answers them with a rhetorical question: "Yes; have you never read: 'Out of the mouth of babes and sucklings...?'" quoting Psalm 8:3. The hosanna prophecy of the Bible is fulfilled. A careful reading of the Bible shows that the life of the Messiah has been foretold in the Old Testament, even to the smallest detail.

Of all the evangelists it is Matthew who delights the most in bringing these details into high relief. A typical expression of his is: "This took place in order to fulfil what had been said by the Lord through the mouth of the prophet" or other such expressions. They sound almost like a refrain. A profound reading of the Old Testament indicates that the Prophet of Nazareth is the centre of Scripture.

On this point Matthew and John are one. John too proclaims the same truth. John describes the calling of the first disciples by Jesus as the fulfilment of the Old Testament. Philip tells Nathanael: "We have found him of whom Moses in the law and also the prophets wrote" (Jn 1:45).

For this disciple the Prophet of Nazareth is the centre of the Scriptures, foretold by Moses and the prophets and the bearer of perfect salvation to Israel, the revealer of divine life.

The passage in Psalm 69 about the zeal for the house of the Lord (v. 10) is fulfilled by the prophetical act of Jesus chasing the merchants from the Temple (Jn 2:17); so too the gift of the true bread from heaven, but not in the manna of Psalm 78:24, rather, in the person and Word of Christ (Jn 6:3). The oracle on the living waters quoted is fulfilled in relation to the person of Jesus (Jn 7:38f). The passages cited in John 12:15 come to their fulfilment in the Master's triumphal entry into Jerusalem. John remarks that these things had been written about him (Jn 12:16).

The parable of the wicked servants in the vineyard, in the last part where Jesus puts across his message, takes up the same theme: reading the Bible (and in particular here Psalm 118:22f) shows that the life of Christ has already been described in the Old Testament. Hence the Master concludes his exposition with a rhetorical question aimed straight at his hearers: "Have you not read this scripture: 'The very stone the builders rejected has become the head of the corner...?'" (Mk 12:10f and parallel texts).

This Old Testament prophecy has enormous value from a Christological point of view, because it contains a summary of the essential elements in the fate of the Messiah, the beloved Son of God (cf. Mk 12:16). Thus the psalmist predicts the Messiah's exaltation, after his rejection by the Jewish people. Careful reading of the prophecy reveals this coming about in what happened to Jesus. Here too, therefore, the Prophet of Nazareth appears to be the centre of the Bible.

A superficial glance over the Old Testament does not see this, but searching the Scriptures (cf. Jn 5:39), which is to say, meditating seriously upon biblical revelation, leads one to the same truth. The Old Testament speaks of Christ, foretelling his coming and his fate: rejection by the human race and exaltation by God.

Hence listening profoundly to the Word, that is, the *lectio divina*, is absolutely vital, and it is important carefully and attentively to meditate upon the Bible, so as to catch and link up all the clues about Christ.

The whole of the Old Testament is one great messianic prophecy. Bearing this in mind, the attentive reader grasps the many elements which make full sense when seen in the light of the life of Jesus, Son of David. The *lectio divina* understood in this way sheds a new light on the Law of Moses, the prophets and the psalms. We see their point, their purpose. There is a great plan of salvation taking place in history whose pinnacle and point of perfection is in the Prophet of Nazareth.

b) *By reading the Bible one finds life*

Each of the synoptic writers records the conversation between Jesus and the scribe about which is the greatest of the commandments (Mk 12:18ff). Only Luke, however, gives our Lord's explicit reference to reading the Bible. Here Jesus says: "What is written in the Law? How do you read it?" (Lk 10:26). The Prophet of Nazareth is speaking to a man who is professionally engaged in the Scriptures; for this reason he is named *nomikos*, a man of the Law (Lk 10:25). Jesus would know well that his interrogator would have meditated on the Scripture each day with the closest of attention. With a finely tuned teaching instinct, Jesus managed to make the scribe give the precise answer to his own question. For the scribe was well aware that the Torah contained the correct norms for living: they are the Lord's commandments, summed up perfectly in the command to love God and one's neighbour. So the Master congratulates the wise reply of the scribe and invites him to make this precept the standard by which to live his life (Lk 10:28).

Jesus is convinced that by reading the Bible with care and attention one can discover the will of God; one can also be stimulated to follow that divine will. Knowing what God demands from his people, the believer is invited to keep the Lord's precepts and have life. Meditating upon the Word day and night, following the psalmist's exhortation, man finds his joy in doing the Law of the Lord (Ps 1:1ff). Hence the Prophet of Nazareth encourages the scribe to do what stands written in the Law; if he does, he will live (Lk 10:28). For the Word is the source of salvation; nourished by it, believers acquire the strength to do the will of God as laid down in the Bible. This is because the Word of God flows from the same power as its author and effects what it proposes in those who read it with care and attention. Hence it should be one of the principal duties of all believers to meditate on the Word. In searching the Scriptures one finds divine life.

c) *Search the Scriptures!*

In the Fourth Gospel we observe how Jesus gives his unbelieving questioners the same command: search the Scriptures and it will become clear that the Prophet of Nazareth is the centre point of the Bible. They will become open to the light of Christ and will adhere to the person of Christ and hence obtain life (Jn 5:31). The structure of this text is one of progressive parallelism; life comes through the Scriptures, salvation comes through Christ. It unfolds as follows:

A) Search *the Scriptures*
B) because you hold the opinion that in them you *have eternal life;*
A') indeed *they* bear witness to me,
B') and you do not wish to come to me to *have life.*

The Old Testament disposes a person to believe in Jesus; Moses and the prophets have written about the Prophet of Nazareth (Jn 1:45); good and well-disposed people like Philip and Nathanael are led to the Messiah by reading the Bible (Jn 1:44-49). It is worth pausing for a moment on "the true Israelite" whom Jesus saw under the fig tree (Jn 1:47f).

If, as several exegetes suggest, his sitting under a fig tree alludes to his study of the Torah, then Nathanael is presented to us as a searcher, a rabbi, one who meditates upon the Scriptures night and day. Here we probably have an allusion to his great love for the Bible: this Israelite was studying the Word of God under the fig tree. Rabbis customarily sat under trees to meditate and teach the Scriptures. In an indirect way Nathanael is depicted as a scribe dedicated to studying the Bible. All the same this true Israelite is one of the few exceptions Jesus meets. Almost all his contemporaries seem

48

unable to search the Scriptures in any profound manner, simply because they are not open in faith nor welcome the person of the Messiah about whom the Scriptures have been written (Jn 5:40-47). An authentic *lectio divina* is beyond them because they are not docile to the action of the Holy Spirit who generates children of God by means of faith (Jn 3:5ff). It is the Spirit who is rightly called the Spirit of truth; he brings people into the fullness of truth (Jn 14:6); that is, he makes them embrace the grace of the truth: the full and perfect revelation of truth in person, the Lord Jesus Christ (Jn 14:6).

d) *The veil that impedes a true* lectio divina

So what prevents Jesus' countrymen from plumbing the depths of the Scriptures? Paul of Tarsus gives us an answer. For many years he was a rabbi of the strict Pharisee observance; he too was a victim of a similar spiritual deficiency; he struggled against Christ, persecuting his followers. For Paul the hearts of the unbelieving Jews are covered with a veil that prevents them from understanding and seeking out the true meaning of the Old Testament (2 Cor 3:14ff). It is like a sort of spiritual cataract making it impossible to see the light and observe what is really happening, except in a confused and shadowy way. In contrast to the Christians who contemplate the glory of God without any veil, these others are not motivated by the Holy Spirit (2 Cor 3:17ff).

For any true *lectio divina*, then, the presence of the Holy Spirit is necessary in order that the eyes of the mind and the heart are opened and made responsive to divine grace. The veil that prevents us reaching the very depths of Scripture is unbelief; that is, when one places oneself beyond the reach of the Holy Spirit who lights up and revives the flame of faith in people to bring them to cling to Christ and his Word.

Clearly such unbelief finds different expressions in practice, from the total absolute refusal in principle to the Gospel down to the daily compromises of everyday Christian living.

Those who positively and wilfully deny the Son of God are totally closed to the influence of the Holy Spirit and are thereby quite unable to listen to what Scripture is really saying.

They might be able to discourse at length on textual and literary criticism in the Bible, but they will never be able to grasp the essential message of the Word. In the same way, too, believers who do not place themselves under the influence of the Spirit will be similarly unable to experience a deep and fruitful *lectio divina.*

2. *Lucan models of the* lectio divina

The New Testament offers us a number of interesting and instructive examples of the *lectio divina.* We will confine ourselves to Luke. He gives us models of the *lectio divina* in both his gospel and in the Acts of the Apostles. He provides us with two incidents when Jesus practised a *lectio divina,* towards the beginning of his ministry (Lk 4:16ff) and towards the end of his physical presence on earth (Lk 24:13). In Acts we find two further examples of *lectio divina,* by Philip the evangelist (Acts 8:26ff) and Paul of Tarsus in the synagogue at Antioch of Pisidia (Acts 13:15ff).

Luke is the evangelist of "listening"; for him the ability to listen is vital. Listening is not only paying attention to the spoken word but also to the written word, proclaimed in the public assembly or read on one's own. Luke gives us paradigms of *lectio divina* in both his books.

a) Lectio divina *in the synagogue at Nazareth*

This is the first of those episodes concerning listening to the Word. It occurs right at the beginning of Jesus' ministry and takes place in the town synagogue (Lk 4:16ff) and describes a liturgical *lectio divina,* the solemn proclamation of the Scriptures in the presence of the assembly. Jesus stands up in the midst of all those taking part and reads a passage from the book of Isaiah.

This is the first thing to notice, the careful and solemn proclamation of the sacred text, in this instance that of Isaiah 61:1. The second step is also briefly traced by Luke: the personal appropriation of the Word into one's life. Jesus applies the word of the prophet to himself. He declares that this text of Isaiah has its full meaning in him: "Today this scripture has been fulfilled."

Luke also gives us the reactions of those present. It is one of utter rejection. The people of Nazareth are unable to take the message of the Word to heart (Lk 4:22ff).

b) *The Risen Lord's way of practising the* lectio divina

At the end of his gospel, Luke gives another way in which Jesus practised the *lectio divina*. It comes in that singular episode of the Risen Lord's appearance to the two disciples on their way to Emmaus (Lk 24:13ff). Christ walks alongside the two disappointed disciples. They are fully resigned to the fate suffered by their Master who has been crucified by the leaders of the Jewish people. They have absolutely no suspicion that Jesus will rise again and so they are leaving Jerusalem in deep grief. They are downcast at the tragic end to the life of the Prophet of Nazareth.

The Master falls in with the two walkers without saying who he is. He becomes involved with their problems which are weighing them down in sorrow. After they describe to him the ignominious death of Christ, the Risen One enters on his own *lectio divina* (Lk 24:25ff).

The first point which Jesus emphasizes when he speaks to them is the need for an open heart in order to enter into the spirit of the message conveyed by the inspired authors of Scripture: "O foolish men, and slow of heart to believe all that the prophets have spoken" (v. 25).

The two disciples on the way to Emmaus do not have the correct attitude of welcome to the Word. They are not reborn in the Holy Spirit; the shaft of the light of faith has not yet illumined their hearts (Jn 3:3ff). That is why they have not grasped that the passion and death of the Messiah are the necessary condition upon which he must enter into glory.

Only after this does the Risen One begin to explain and make clear the Scriptures about the Christ, beginning with Moses (Lk 24:27). This outlines in summary form the first stage of the *lectio divina*: it consists in reading and reflecting deeply upon the text with the assistance of an accurate exegesis. In this scene Jesus is described as the true interpreter of Scripture, in whom the reality of Scripture comes to life.

The comment of the two disciples after the Risen One has explained to them: "Did not our hearts burn within us while he talked to us on the road, while he opened to us the Scriptures?" (v. 32) illustrates beautifully the stage of attentive listening in the *lectio divina*. This is the moment when faith and love are revived; men and women are transformed by the divine message. Here we have a model that can stimulate our own *lectio divina*. For Luke shows how the Word, when it is read or heard, must transform the human heart. We are taught in this way how we can become pupils of Jesus.

First of all, it is important for any fruitful *lectio divina* to struggle against a hardening of the heart. *Sklerokardia* is a constant menace when it comes to grasping the deep meaning of Scripture; this hardening of the heart prevents us from understanding and living the Word. Who can help us in this struggle? The Spirit of the Lord, who creates a new heart in us, one which is sensitive to the message of Scripture. So before even beginning to listen to the Word, one needs to invoke the assistance of the Holy Spirit. Secondly, the Bible needs explaining. In Luke 24:27 we see Jesus in person is the true interpreter.

In the *lectio divina* the believer must use every available tool of biblical science at his or her disposal. Thirdly, listening effectively to the Word focuses our attention on the person of Jesus. The Old Testament speaks of Jesus, the prophet of Nazareth, as truly the centre of the Bible. This is a vital hermeneutical key to the Scriptures. It does not betray or distort the literal meaning of the Old Testament prophecies, but it leads us to a deeper understanding of the text and holds together the unity of all Scripture.

Finally, all *lectio divina* is intended to make our hearts burn. The natural and most enjoyable fruits of all listening to the Word are prayer and contemplation. The disciples on the way to Emmaus experienced such heights because they were transformed by the risen Christ. Yet all believers can experience the same if only they let themselves be guided by the Holy Spirit.

c) *The deacon Philip's* lectio divina *with the Ethiopian*

In the Acts of the Apostles, Luke lays before us another example of the *lectio divina*, that of Philip and the Ethiopian (Acts 8:26-40). It is one of the most stimulating examples in the Book of Acts.

The Ethiopian, a powerful minister of Queen Cadace, is returning home from Jerusalem. He is reading the prophet Isaiah, to be precise, the fourth song of the Suffering Servant of the Lord (Is 52:13ff). The eunuch is reading the Scripture but is having no success with a *lectio divina* since he cannot understand the prophecies (Acts 8:34). Clearly he does not possess the Holy Spirit. Philip, on the other hand, inspired by the Spirit of the Lord (cf. Acts 8:29.39), assists the Ethiopian in discovering the true meaning of the passage he is reading by relating it to Jesus, the Prophet of Nazareth. So effective is this *lectio divina* that the eunuch is converted to Christ and desires to be baptized in the name of the Lord Jesus (Acts 8:36ff).

Here we find a description in summary of the basic stages of the *lectio divina*. Initially one aligns oneself with the Holy Spirit; true, this is only hinted at, but it is a vital requirement. Next, quite clearly comes the reading and explanation of the text; the Ethiopian reads aloud and Philip interprets the divine prophecy. Finally, one comes to realize that the passage not only contains the understanding of prophecy in the light of Christ, but it points to the completing phase where the one is totally transformed and becomes a real disciple of Christ.

d) *The* lectio divina *in the synagogue at Antioch*

In his gospel we have seen Luke describing a liturgical setting of the *lectio divina*, presided over by Jesus in the synagogue at Nazareth (Lk 4:16ff).

In Acts we find a similar synagogal liturgy held on a Sabbath at Antioch in Pisidia (Acts 13:13ff). Present are Paul and Barnabas. The liturgy is made up of readings, commentary on the Law of Moses and the Prophets. This particular passage tells us nothing about which readings were used; nor is it possible to deduce anything from Paul's subsequent speech, since this appears to be a synopsis of the history of Israel, from the time of the election of the Patriarchs to the choice of David (Acts 13:17-22). Paul speaks in this way in order to present the Gospel, the Good News, which is centred upon the descendant of David: the Saviour Jesus Christ (Acts 13:23ff).

What is certain and interests us is the way in which the liturgy unfolds. It has two essential stages: (i) the solemn reading of Scripture, and (ii) the application of Scripture to the present time, once it has been interpreted. This is the very kernel of the *lectio divina*. There is also the important, though implicit, element for understanding the Bible in its deep meaning: to be in harmony with Scripture through the Holy Spirit. Paul is able to penetrate the Word of God and interpret it correctly in a Christological perspective because he is filled with the Holy Spirit (Acts 13:9).

Chapter 4

The *lectio divina* in Eastern monastic tradition

Jean Gribomont

Right from the very beginning of monasticism we find instances and sayings that seek to stimulate zeal for the inspired Scriptures; at the same time we can find consolation for those humble souls who feel themselves incapable of such a reading. For the desire for purity of heart and a life lived in the presence of God without any distractions, observing his commandments, which the Word frequently encourages, found expression in the beginning in rather uncultivated surroundings, where intellectual activity held little attraction. Far from having literary aspirations, it seems that the monks were guided by a return to untamed nature, without roof or fire or clothing, where silence brings man once again close to the animal kingdom. Certainly this is something of a caricature; we do find some teachers of a gnostic tendency who are the heirs of Origen, the Stoics, Pythagoreans and Porphyrians. They all profess a sincere respect for the Bible, though it is a matter of some interest how they practise this.

1. *Radical poverty*

Thus there are hermits in the deserts of Egypt and in Syria, the eccentric wonder-workers described by Theodoretus, in whose hands it is difficult to imagine even a minimum of books. The *Apophthegmata Patrum* recounts that Theodore of Fermete (*Alphabeticon*, n. 1) possessed three beautiful

55

books; the Abbot Macarios, while acknowledging the benefit he and the other brothers might draw from them, coun-
selled him to sell them and give the money to the poor.
Serapion was even less polite:

> You have taken the possessions of the widows and the poor and put
> them on this shelf full of books (*Alphabeticon*, n. 2).

Gelasius owned a complete Bible. It was worth eighteen
pieces of silver (*Alphabeticon*, n. 1). He had it put in the
church for the use of the brothers. When it was stolen he was
careful not to worry about recovering it.

Another *apophthegm*, but not so ancient describes a
brother who had dedicated himself to reading night and day
for twenty years giving up his books and retiring to the
desert, saying to Abbot Isaac: "For twenty years I have done
nothing but listen to the Word of Scriptures, now at last I
want to dedicate myself to doing the works I have heard
about in the Scriptures."

This attitude is typical of a mind-set more interested in
effectively conforming to the Word of God than in *dilettante*
study. Today our educational system and culture incline us
to be huge consumers of the written word; our memories no
longer absorb and retain things in the same way because they
are distracted by so many stimuli. But a word captured in the
liturgy, repeated again and again in solitude, at work, in
prayer, can have a quite different effect, especially when it is
received as the Word of God guiding all formation of conscience and the point of reference in every situation in life.
Over-concentration on one text can cause difficulties too;
that is why the liturgy is so beneficial with its alternating
texts of epistles, gospels, psalms and wisdom texts over a
stated period, and, in any case, this helps to prevent the
exaggerated growth of false interpretations or the isolation
of one particular truth.

Nevertheless, there is many a lesson for us today from
authentic monasticism such as discretion in human curiosity
about God's Word and in all intellectual craving; likewise a

radical putting into second place of the need for novelty, so that attention is given to what is central, an impressive recognition of what is essential as a result of the poverty of silence in the desert. Earthly wisdom does not naturally reach these heights; consequently, it is useful for us to look towards the example of enduring patience in a *staretz*, poor in spirit, meek of heart.

One can find some unexpected examples of this renunciation of reading Sacred Scripture, and even in Basil, who was also concerned to search the Scriptures, to make of them a rule for the whole Church. In the *Asceticon*, the Small Rule (n. 235) asks whether it is suitable to learn lots of things (*polla ekmanein*) from the Scriptures. It is interesting that the question even arises. Unreserved encouragement is taken for granted. But the spokesman for the Bible is no doubt aware of a small local conflict, in which the losing side is appealing for his agreement; he is very careful not to commit himself with his eyes shut:

> There are, in conclusion, two categories (*tagmata*) of people: those entrusted with the responsibility of guiding and those in a position of trusting and being obedient; both have their charism. In my opinion, however, he who presides and holds overall responsibility should know what is the overall need, carefully learning so as to teach everyone what it is that God desires... As regards the others, each should be mindful of what the Apostle says: "Do not overestimate yourself more than it is suitable. Each of you must judge himself soberly (*hyperphronei, phronei, sôphionein*) by the standard of the faith God has given him" (Rom 12:13). So learn and be eager to do what is worthy of God who has said: "Well done, good and faithful servant; you have shown you can be faithful over a little, I will set you over much" (Mt 25:21).

The subsequent question recommends all who are privileged to study the four gospels to benefit from the privilege.

As a young and zealous convert, Basil had invited his readers to join him in criticizing those biblical authorities who taught less than the whole truth. I do not believe that he ever gave up this reforming radicalism. In these replies, he is thinking of more than community discipline. Without doubt he is thinking of the attitudes of those brothers who would have claimed the right to take their place with those who were qualified to study. In the first place, it is a good thing to teach in the communion of brotherhood with the humble confidence (*eupeitheia*) that allows for the diversity of charisms. Despite this restrictive text's isolation within Basil's works, it does uphold, in his particular way, the privilege of poverty of the Egyptian monks.

2. *The libraries*

In the monasteries, poverty was never an insuperable obstacle to the building up of libraries. We know of typical collections at Mount Athos, Mount Sinai, in Syria and in Constantinople, among the Acemites, which it would take time to describe. In Egypt there was the White Monastery, Our Lady of the Syrians. It is quite possible that the Pachomian monks buried their gnostic books at Nag Hammadi so as not to incur the wrath of overzealous censors. But no catalogues of the resources and exegetical interests have come down to us from those first centuries.

Clearly it was the educated monks who left their mark. We know that Jerome, after his conversion, gathered together a library. He does not list the Bible; there would be no need for that; he mentions Hilary. Still we can be assured that his library would have consisted of the religious and profane writings which he constantly used. In his younger years he often borrowed volumes in Hebrew; later he settled down close to the exceptional library at Caesarea which contained the works of Origen, Pamphilus, Eusebius and Acacius, and those who followed them.

A short distance from Caesarea, at Jerusalem, beside Melania, Rufinus built a shop for Greek books, which he took and translated in the West. It would be fascinating to know how the Cappadocians supplied themselves with books. Some who still attribute to Basil and Gregory of Nazianzus the compilation of the *Philokalia* of Origen, as they were first studying theology, are of the opinion they had a wide selection. The documentation which Basil can conjure up from the first centuries concerning the Holy Spirit would suggest, either in the episcopal palace at Caesarea or in the fraternity beside it, a wonderful patrology, to which Gregory of Nyssa himself would contribute at least one copy of Philo. Evagrius Ponticus, a scribe by profession, certainly collected a whole library of Pythagorean writings, not to mention Christian ones. It is amazing that we do not know more about the transfer of books between these centres; but no one who visited Didymus of Alexandria – whatever were the Blind Man's contacts with the intellectual movements around him – went away without receiving something from him.

When Basil looked for support from the newly-elected Archbishop of Milan, Ambrose, it is perfectly reasonable to surmise that he would entrust his messengers with a parcel of books, traces of which can be found in the homilies of Ambrose. Indeed, it is this rather educated élite, admirers of and to a certain extent the products of monasticism, who were the protagonists of the exchange of ideas. They did not hesitate to use the wisdom of the ascetics and some pagan mysticism, always with the proviso that everything be subject to the orthodoxy of the sacred books.

The coenobitic life was more suited to the diffusion of books than the eremetical life. The *Precepts of Pachomius* (n. 25) give permission to borrow a book for a week; further on (nn. 100-101) great care of books is recommended and that they be replaced in their correct position by evening; such love is a good sign.

3. *Meditation*

The *lectio divina*, however, was not an affair purely of books. One of the first duties of the hermit, as for the coenobitic monk, was to commit to memory the Psalter, the

New Testament, and on occasions, other things as well. Between periods of work, movement and meals, the devout musings of the monks would bring to mind and tongue these familiar formulae; this was known as *meditatio*. The tradition, as we know, has developed more by concentrating upon a single, fundamental formula, such as the Jesus Prayer or, as in the West, the Rosary. The relative merits of both practices are a matter of some debate. The rather mechanical reciting from the inspired books did have the effect of drawing attention to and inculcating the spirit of the Gospel themes, even though it was not able to combine the simplicity and intensity of ecstatic prayer.

It is in the Pachomean *koinonia* that we find the best-attested practice of reflecting on the Scriptures. There are still extant Coptic fragments, in Latin translations made by Jerome, of several well-known instructions by Pachomius, echoing his meditation. The works of Pachomius and his successors, Orsisius and Theodorus, are hardly works of logical argument but rather a patchwork of quotations from the Old Testament in particular, and especially the Wisdom literature. The monitions apply these biblical references very concretely to the life of the community; the authors communicate their understanding of rebukes and invitations by the men of God in order to lead their brothers to an edifying interpretation.

There is one charming example of this, recalled by Theodorus when he was a young monk in a different community, concerning the teaching of Pachomius. It comes courtesy of a fellow-monk who had to stay overnight at Tabennisi. The recollection has been included in the principal life of Pachomius, paragraph 29 in the Coptic version and paragraph 34 in the first Greek version. The monk travelling from the north subsequently recounts to the young Theodorus:

Pachomius was sitting and speaking the Word of God to the assembled brothers. He spoke of the Tabernacle and the Holy of Holies, applying these to the two peoples. The first is the outer tabernacle, whose sacrifices consist in visible sacrifices; the Holy of Holies, on the other hand, is the call to the nations, the fullness of the Law (Rom 13:10). Everything that is found in this inner tabernacle is complete in glory; instead of animal sacrifice, there is an altar of incense; instead of the table, the ark with the spiritual loaves; replacing the light from the lampstand, the propitiation which has the appearance of a consuming fire, God (Heb 12:29), rather, the Word made man (Jn 1:14) who became forgiveness for sins when he was made visible in the flesh (1 Tim 3:16).

This theme, selected and emphasized by the filial devotion of Theodorus, is one of exceptional quality. It sums up the relationship between the monastic ideal and Egyptian Christian worship, an ideal which the Letter to the Hebrews casts in the relationship between the Levitical and the New Covenant. It is an adaptation that is as orthodox as possible of Origenist gnosis to the conditions of the fourth century. Each individual listener is quite sensitive to the way in which sacramental practice is here being spiritualized; but there is no other purpose behind it than realizing through monastic ascetism the full teaching of Paul and John.

Not all the catechesis that have come down to us, and the meditations that presuppose them, attain to such a spiritual level. Nonetheless, they display an extraordinary finesse of spirit, in a part of the Western world devoid of a theological academy and where Greek culture was infiltrating via the liturgy and other contacts; that spirit seems to have been cultivated both from the Scriptures as well as the experience of a life of grace.

4. Reading and history

The extract of spiritual exegesis quoted above opens up the question of the different methods of Scriptural exegesis in monastic circles, literal, allegorical and the like.

If the library discovered at Nag Hammadi does belong to a Pachomean community, then it is reasonable to suppose in some a highly developed curiosity, more than one would believe from reading about the lives and ways of behaviour in Coptic circles.

Furthermore, even if the monks were not necessarily totally gnostic, and if librarians then, like the librarians of today, accumulated most what was of contemporary interest (except where they had to be careful not to incur the wrath of their less liberal-minded superiors), it seems to be generally agreed that in the time of Pachomius one could read, in Copt, more adventurous ideas than those put forward by Origen, Didymus or even Evagrius.

The classical sources of monasticism are clearly anti-Origen, with a tendency to simplify which seem to exclude totally the exegesis of Evagrius and his disciples. These sources, however, only represent what has been conserved after the violent upheavals of the fourth century in the time of Theophilus.

The fact that they are eminently conservative and orthodox might suggest that they had been radically censored. Anthony's letters, which I believe to be genuine, are naïvely Origenist; but these have been preserved thanks to their Arab or Georgian editions.

The variety of monastic literature differs according to the personalities, level of culture and differing periods. Two brothers such as Basil and Gregory of Nyssa, for example, can relate each in his own different way to the Old and New Testaments and to Philo and Origen; culture and spritual-mindedness are not the same thing.

The same author can switch styles at will, respecting both the literary form of the biblical book subject to commentary and the literary genre he is using, as well as the public he hopes to edify. Basil's homilies on the psalms, for example, are much more Origenist than those on the *Esameron*; the homilies on the gospel texts are quite different again.

Apart from the Pachomean writers who quote more often than comment on the Scriptures, and the Basilean *Asceticon*, which is based entirely on the New Testament, the literature directed to monks shows little signs of biblical development.

An *apophthegm* of Poemen (*Alphabeticon*, 8) is typical. Poemen received a visit from an anchorite from afar who was waiting for great spiritual wisdom.

They greeted each other warmly. But when the anchorite, quoting Scripture, began to speak of spiritual and heavenly things, Poemen turned away. The other, quite dismayed, began to reproach his brother for not even speaking to him after he had travelled such a long way. The aged Poemen explained:

> You are from on high and speak of spiritual things; I am of below and speak of earthly things. Had you spoken of the passions of the heart I might have replied.

The stranger ended up understanding the reason why the old man had not spoken willingly from the Scriptures and left "very uplifted". This same Poemen elsewhere counsels:

> If you cannot keep silent, it is better to speak about the sayings of the elders than about Scripture; because in the latter there is no little danger (*Amon*, 2).

There are only a few Fathers who make a studied use of allegory; at the same time it is also true to say that very few have a sufficiently good historical formation to be able to situate the Apostles and the Prophets in their times in the strictly literal sense. Of course, a mind as cultivated as Basil can do this quite naturally. He hardly ever quotes a text without first placing it in its context, as a controlling factor in his argumentation.

More often than not, however, the monks adopt a purely psychological approach, bypassing all allegory and going straight to the original circumstances of the text's formulation. Though the hermeneutic be oversimplified, it is not necessarily falsified; a well-formed conscience can easily discern the drift of the meaning of the sacred examples. The background of spiritual experience, a humility before the divine mysteries, a respect for tradition, can assure a degree of perception which is as valuable as any erudition.

Conclusion

I have tried to concentrate on the original witness of the first "basic communities" (among which one might include those of Basil). Obviously much more could be added were one to include Athanasius, the classical works of the Cappadocians, and still more Jerome – the professional of the *lectio divina* – or Didymus and the Antiochene masters. Each one of these is worthy of a chapter, but there already are sufficient works of considerable merit to consult.

Over the ages, certain hours of the monastic day became specifically set apart for reading, others for work, others for singing psalms, according to different patterns: "May the sun, as it rises, find you with a book in your hands" (Evagrius, *Mirror of the Virgins*, 4). The monastic rules regulate this in accordance with the seasons. Certain temptations incite a reaction:

> When the intellect wanders, let reading pin it down, with watching and praying (Evagrius, *Practicos*, 15).

Perhaps the mediaeval Western monk more than his Greek counterpart has stressed the importance of a devout reading, calling to mind that beautiful expression *"solus in angulo cum libello"* – "alone in a quiet corner with a book". Modern Western monasticism has perpetuated the myth, and at times even realized it, of the scholarly monk, the library mouse. Such an ideal would have been quite exceptional in the fourth century, though at Bethlehem Jerome and his spiritual daughters do provide an example. Evagrius, himself an intellectual, quoted Abbot Anthony, much admired by a philosopher for his perseverance in spite of his lack of books. With higher wisdom, the saint had replied:

> My book is creation and it is always open when I want to read the words of God (*Practicos*, 92).

When all is said and done, however, this sentiment does not quite exactly capture the balance between meditation and silence. We might be nearer the Christian sense of things were we to quote from a letter of Basil. After he has commended *hesychasm*, or inner contemplation, and before speaking about prayer, the young convert to the monastic life lays out his thinking on reading:

> The main way to discover our duty is to study the inspired Scriptures of God. In them we find the norms that guide the conduct and the life of holy men... Just as a painter fixes his gaze on what he is copying and tries to transfer all its characteristics to his own work, so too he who would be perfect needs to fix his sight on the lives of the saints and apply them to himself by imitating their goodness. Prayers, when they follow upon reading, find the soul younger and more vigorous.

Chapter 5

Daily reading in the monasteries
(300-700 AD)

Adalbert de Vogüé

1. *The content*

Over the past ten years the expression *lectio divina* has come back into currency. In our own time, it is used mainly to designate the period of spiritual reading in the monk's daily routine.

a) *Reading the Bible*

Even so, most often in ancient times the expression meant something else: the text of Scripture itself. *Lectio* could mean what was read as well as the simple act of reading. In ancient times the first sense was the more common. The "divine reading" was the Bible. In the one passage from the Rule where St Benedict uses the expression (*Rule of St Benedict* [RB] 48,1) the words "to be occupied... in *lectio divina*" (as opposed to manual labour) undoubtedly mean the act of reading, but with a specific objective; one reads the divine books, the Scriptures.

b) *Reading commentaries*

Does this exclude all other books? Benedict requires that not only the Old and New Testaments but also the patristic commentaries on the sacred text be read in the Office (RB 9,8). One can assume that the same freedom is allowed in private reading; side by side with the Bible there are the commentaries of the Fathers. Nevertheless, the objective is strictly scriptural.

Recourse to commentaries is not always regarded either as necessary or opportune. In one lovely text from the *Institutions* (vv. 33-34), Cassian echoes an Egyptian master, Abbot Theodorus, for whom the understanding of Scripture comes less from commentaries and more from purity of heart. Nevertheless, a century and a half later, Cassiodorus will be placing at the disposal of the monks all the commentaries of the Fathers he can find and recommending them heartily. One senses there something of that zeal which caused him not only to furnish the monastery with a patristic library for the *lectio divina* but also his sense of intellectual curiosity in founding the monastery of Vivarium. Contemporary witnesses to Benedict attest that the same need was widely felt throughout the monasticism of his time.

c) *Pagan culture: help or hindrance?*

Cassiodorus's ambitions followed the direction of Augustine in *De Doctrina Christiana*. He considered it vital to cultivate the secular sciences in order to understand the Word of God better. In this he stands in stark contrast to Cassian who never mentions pagan culture – by which he meant literature more than the sciences – except as an impediment to prayer (*Confessiones* XIV, 12-13). The change in attitude came about largely through the decline in culture: in the time of Cassiodorus it was no longer knowledge which proved dangerous but ignorance. Towards the end of the sixth century, Pope Gregory, though maintaining on several occasions his aversion to secular literature, nevertheless recognizes their indispensable role as an aid to understanding Scripture (*In Regum* V, 83-85).

As far as Benedict is concerned, however, because of his absolute silence on the question, it is impossible to attribute to him any view on the subject. What does seem certain is that the hours prescribed in the Rule for reading are intended for reading the Bible or those Christian writings and authors directly illuminating it.

2. *The timing*

It is foreseen in the Rule that reading will occupy in all about three hours of the day. In Lent, which is a time of special spiritual commitment, Benedict lays down that the three-hour reading be continuous. For the remainder of the year it is more broken up, one might even say complicated. Generally the monastic rules assign reading to one of the four periods of three hours which went to make up the ancient day-span; the rest of the time was set aside for manual work, daily business and meals. Only Sunday, the day when no work is done, is completely given over to reading.

a) *The three hours of daily reading*

The principle of three hours daily reading, at times reduced to two (or, in the case of women, to one hour but with compensatory duties) appears almost from the very beginnings of Western monastic literature, that is, from about the year 400. We find this principle in two very old rules which have come down to our day; the Augustinian *Ordo Monasterii*, ca. 395, and the *Rule of the Four Fathers*, about a decade or so later.

The *Ordo* appoints the reading to take place from the sixth to the ninth hour (from 12 noon to 3 o'clock). The *Four Fathers* puts it from the first to the third hour (from 6 to 9 o'clock). The differences are less important than the consensus of these early formulations, apparently independent of one another, on the length of time assigned to reading on working days. Why are the monks of Africa and Gaul, followed in succeeding centuries by those in Italy and Spain, all in agreement about this quantity of time inserted into their daily timetable?

The way in which the monks divided the day in the West appears to have been very much an innovation. Neither Pachomius nor Basil had envisaged in their legislation special times for *lectio divina*; we can hardly suppose that Basil, whose draft version of a Rule is contained in a letter to Gregory of Nazianzus (Ep. 2,3-4) had in mind the final hours of the day. Jerome, describing the coenobitic monks of Egypt (Ep. 22,35,7) in 384, confines himself to stating that the monks begin their day by fulfilling their allotted work, which allows them the rest of the day for *oratio* and *lectio*. Here too reading is done after work but without any set duration.

It was quite an innovation then in Western monasteries to establish a fixed time of three hours to be reserved for reading. This norm appears to be an attempt to steer between contrasting practices: incessant work and absenteeism from work. In the Egyptian monasteries described by Cassian, the brothers are taken up with work from morning till night; their manual labour is accompanied by meditation and punctuated with ejaculatory prayers; neither the Rule of Pachomius nor the *Institutions* refer to any pause from work in order to read. In Gaul, on the other hand, in the last quarter of the fourth century, the followers of Martin of Tours "attend to prayer" the whole of the day; only the younger monks do manual work, and even this is of a rather superior kind – copying manuscripts. Similarly at Carthage in the year 400, the monks, who seem to have come from the East and whom Augustine criticizes in *De Opere Monachorum*, imagine they may do nothing other than reading and praying.

Between these two extremes, of total inaction – reminiscent of the Messalians of Syria – and of incessant activity – ascribed by Cassian to the monks of Egypt – the Latin monks adopted a formula which was balanced. They assigned a limited time to spiritual activity, two or three times less than that envisaged for manual work, but nonetheless important enough to constitute a fine homage to the Lord. To forego in this way each day three hours of productive labour in order

70

to dedicate oneself to a selfless occupation is no mean sacrifice; it affirms the primacy of the spiritual. In the view of Augustine the financial loss incurred justifies the request for contributions from the faithful (*De Opere Monachorum*, 20). It is not through accumulating this world's goods but in their attachment to the Word of God that the monks have honour.

b) *The position of the three hours in the day*

The length of time given to the *lectio* is not the only issue worthy of consideration. Its time-tabling is just as significant. In the ancient documents there appears to have been three quite distinct systems, each subject to its own inner logic.

As Jerome remarked, beginning the *lectio* after one's *pensum* or daily work is to make the point that once the minimum subsistence has been secured then all that remains belongs to the spirit and to God.

To practise the *lectio* in the middle of the day, before the main meal at None (*Ordo Monasterii*), emphasizes the sustenance of the spirit before the body. It is giving reading the prime time of the day when the stomach is empty and the spirit is light and free and joyfully disposed to prayer. When the *lectio* takes place in the morning, before any work is begun (*Rule of the Four Fathers*), this is a reminder that nothing must prevent or curtail this capital exercise. It endows the *lectio* with a freshness and exclusivity free as yet from daily distractions.

This last system deserves closer attention since Pelagius in his letter to Demetridos (para. 23) makes express reference to its point and purposes. These three hours are "the better part" offered up to God. Later, too, in Western monasticism the practice will be adopted universally, taking into account seasonal variations. Finally, and perhaps most importantly, this system provides us with an important glimpse into the ancient Christian past.

c) *The origins of the morning reading*

One can go back to about the year 200, the time of the *Apostolic Tradition* of Hippolytus (para. 41) to see that the Christian is exhorted to read privately, at home, at daybreak on those days when there is no Christian morning assembly. Even though it is not explicitly mentioned that reading should last until the third hour, the sudden mention of this hour immediately after this counsel makes one naturally take it as an invitation to read for three hours. Indeed, some two centuries later, the *De Virginitate*, attributed to Anastasius, enjoins all religiously consecrated virgins to read from the first to the third hour (para. 12). Evagrius Ponticus lays down in almost identical language the same rule in the *Sentences to Virgins* (n. 4) though the reading concludes on the second hour.

The Spanish nun, Egeria, a little time before (381-384), testifies to a rather remarkable practice in Jerusalem. Throughout the whole of Lent, the bishop prepared the candidates who were to be baptized at Easter, with catechetical assemblies from the first to the third hour (*Journal* 46,3). These assemblies, in which primacy was given to reading and interpreting first of the Scriptures, then of the Creed, were composed not only of catechumens but also of those faithful who desired to attend and had the possibility to do so – and doubtlessly there would have been no shortage of these in one of the great pilgrimage centres of the world, in which there were many monks. All of them, men and women alike, were there for some weeks taking part in a kind of retreat or renewal, reading and deepening the great foundational texts of the Christian faith together with the bishop and the *competentes*.

d) *The yearly renewal of faith through the* lectio divina

The Jerusalem Lenten community *lectio divina* undoubtedly influenced many pilgrims and contributed to the sudden and widespread growth of the three-hour reading at the beginning of the day from about the year 400. We have already seen that attested: in Palestine by Pelagius, in Egypt by Evagrius, elsewhere in the East by the Pseudo-Athanasius and in the West by the four Fathers. We might add along with these, though they are not so precise about how long it should take, John Chrysostom (*Homiliae in 1 Tim.*, 14,4) and Isaiah of Scetos (*Logos* 3,42).

One can see now, in the light of Egeria's report, the significance of the monastic practice of reading before Terce. The monks do daily what in Jerusalem was done annually. "At every moment", writes Benedict, "the life of the monk should be lived with the same intensity as in Lent" (RB 49,1). This is what happened in point of fact. What was a Lenten practice came to be extended to the whole year. Each morning, throughout the ages, monks and nuns begin their day by listening to the Word of God in which their faith in Christ is renewed and their love for him deepened.

3. *Various situations and points of reference with regard to the* lectio

The same sort of communitarian catechesis as found in Jerusalem is not so distant, as one might believe, from that practised in the monasteries.

a) *Communitarian and private* lectio

While the Rule of St Benedict gives the impression that the *lectio* is done, as it is today, by each monk individually, the Rule of the Master [RM], to which it is close, envisages only a communitarian *lectio*. Only one in ten reads in the group; the others listen. Moreover, the Benedictine Rule conserves a trace of this practice. The "Instrument of Good Works", drawn from the Spiritual Art of the Master, commands "listening willingly to holy writings" (RB 4,55 and RM 3,61).

b) *Prattling and praying*

This regulation is not only interesting from the point of view of reading in communities where books are at a premium or where the brothers are unable to read. It is worth looking at in its own right. It is part of a wider context.

"Listening willingly to holy writings", the advice of the Spiritual Art, comes after a series of articles on the use of words and before an article on prayer. They give a key role to *lectio* in asceticism and the spiritual life of the monk.

The preceding sayings, in fact, castigate a number of abuses of the word: speaking too much, speaking for amusement, laughing loudly and too easily. The sayings which come afterwards invite "frequent prostrations in prayer". This then is the setting for "listening willingly to holy writings". By stopping the wrong use of speech, reading prepares the monk to speak devoutly. By listening attentively to the divine Word one goes from sinful human conversation to the holy word that addresses God.

c) *Silence and reading*

The relationship between silence and reading on the one hand and prayer on the other is mentioned often in the writings of antiquity. The Master, who drew up the list of sayings, advises silence before reading takes place among a group of brothers working together. The point is to avoid sinning through gossiping. Idle talk appears to be, in the Sermons of Caesar of Arles, the greatest obstacle to a fruitful reading of the Scriptures both in the church and at home. Silence and reading go hand in hand. One needs silence in order to hear what is being read; reading is one of the best ways too of obtaining silence.

d) *Reading and prayer*

The connection between reading and prayer is clear for all to see. Long before monasticism there is the magnificent statement of St Cyprian which later Fathers never tire of repeating: "Never cease from praying and reading", he advises a new convert. "In prayer you are speaking to God; in reading God is speaking to you."

Following this line of thought, Ambrose, Augustine and Isidore of Seville and others reverse the terms, not without good reason. Usually reading precedes prayer. For in the dialogue between God and man the initiative lies with God, as in the whole story of salvation. It is not we who have first loved; it is God. That is why it is fitting to listen. Our prayer is our response to his voice.

We find this normal order in the Master and Benedict; reading comes before and generates prayer. Both these "tools" sum up admirably the ancient monastic way of praying. This is simply listening to God in the words of Scripture and responding to him in prayer.

e) *Reading and meditation*

Since prayer must be continuous – "pray without ceasing" – then it follows that listening to the divine words must never cease. That is why reading, which lasts for only three hours, needs extending during the rest of the day by meditation. "To meditate" is to repeat over and over again a text which is known by heart. Once the *lectio* is completed, the monk can continue to listen to God because he never ceases to recite the texts of Scripture which are engraved on his memory. This recitation can be done always and everywhere, at work, in all comings and goings, in free times and pauses.

The monk is like a ruminating animal which, according to the Bible, is the only kind of animal that is pure (Lev 11:3; Deut 14:6). He is like that modern labourer always going around with his transistor: in the midst of everything he keeps in touch with a voice that comes from afar; in the case of the modern labourer it is keeping in touch with the world; with the monk it is keeping in touch with God.

Daily reading links up not only with silence and prayer but even more with meditation. One of the purposes of the three-hour reading period is to learn the texts by heart so as to be able to recite them off. A considerable part of the time is given over to this process of memorization. No matter how mechanical it might seem, it diminishes in no way the benefits of the *lectio*. Quite the contrary, for only when a text is known by heart, is it possible to have its full benefits. Meditation does not just extend reading; it makes full use of it and allows it to bear fruit.

f) *A unifying dialogue*

By means of this kind of meditation, reading can become a way of constantly listening to God, which gives rise to more or less long and regular times of prayer.

Thus the whole life of the monk is a dialogue with the Lord. The Divine Office mirrors this same unending rhythmic dialogue of listening and responding, composed of alternating psalms and prayers. And in the first place it consists in listening to God who speaks through the sacred texts and taking from them the material for silent prayer. Thus the *mon*astic life makes its own name come true; from morning till night, behind the diversity of occupations and exercises, it is perfectly "one".

g) *Reading, compunction and conversion*

Finally there is the link of reading to compunction and conversion. Benedict, in the wake of the Master, alludes to it in his catalogue of good works and then mentions it quite independently in the chapter on Lent.

Both the maxims: "Listening willingly to holy writings" and "Prostrate yourself frequently in prayer" are followed by a sentence which commends prayer with tears. This is where the monk confesses his past sins to God and embarks on the process of correcting those self-same sins (RB 13,4; 57-58:

RM 3,63-64). Because of the *lectio* we have gone from idle chatter, not just to prayer but indeed to the transformation of the heart and to corrected behaviour.

Lent, in Benedict's view, is a time for spiritual effort including the wiping out of every vice through "prayer with tears, reading and contrition of heart" (RB 49,4). This association of reading and compunction reminds one of that wonderful text in the Acts of the Apostles which is fundamental for all reflection on "contrition of heart", namely, the Pentecost scene. Peter has just finished speaking to the Jews. Luke states: "They were cut to the heart" (*compuncti sunt corde*). The Jews ask the Apostles what they should do: "Repent..." was the reply.

Just as the Word of God, proclaimed by Peter, touched the hearts of his listeners, so it ought to touch the heart of the monk who hears it in the *lectio divina*. This "cut" or wound of compunction is to be expected from the readings; and its effect is conversion, as recorded in Acts. After the *lectio*, then, the monk will be converted through his contrition. Benedict's "Abstain from every vice", mentioned immediately before, is in fact a programme of conversion, just as the "tears" of prayer, likewise mentioned in this sentence, are the classic signs of contrition of heart.

h) *Reading and contemplation*

The daily reading then of the monks is a way of leading to contrition of heart, tears, conversion. These are highly desirable, even if not habitual. Benedict is not the only one to commend them. Cassian, before him, had associated reading and contrition of heart (*Inst.* V, 14,1) more particularly with the psalms "to maintain unceasingly compunction" (*Confessiones* 17,2). After Benedict, Gregory the Great in a beautiful passage from the *Dialogues* (IV, 49,14,1) tells the story of a monk from his own community on Monte Celio, called Anthony, who "used to repeat over and over the words of Holy Scripture with great fervour and passion, not seeking words of theology but tears of compunction, because only thus can the soul be roused, impassioned and leave this base world to be borne by contemplation to the heavenly homeland."

Compunction prepares us not only for conversion but contemplation. Gregory recalls for us this classical teaching which is based on experience and here opens up new and boundless horizons. Reading prepares us for contemplation and lifts our gaze beyond our existing horizons and reawakens in us the desire for eternal life.

4. *Difficulties with the* lectio

We have travelled the magnificent trails that lead from the *lectio divina*. All the same no one should imagine that monks have always practised the *lectio* with delight and enthusiasm. It might be good for us to conclude by enumerating some of the very human difficulties encountered. Spending three hours face to face with the Bible every day was no easier in the past than it is today, though for vastly different reasons.

The high recommendations of those ancient spokesmen of the past about the *lectio divina* seem to suggest the enormous effort it implied. In a chapter on prayer, Benedict uses two words in an apparently contrasting way: *vacare* (RB 48,4) and *intendere* (RB 48,18). The former, *vacare*, evokes a time of rest – and indeed, reading does presuppose a cessation of manual work; but what is harder for a man than to break off his work and the activities dear to him for something whose results cannot be seen? The second word, *intendere*, means to pay attention to; this word sums up the application that is required in all reading, the true "spiritual work", in the words of the Master (RM 50,16).

Benedict says little about the application involved in reading; he merely deplores its absence among certain monks. In Lent one reads for three hours at a time and there are some brothers, caught in the grip of sloth, who find this too much and begin to gossip among themselves with other like-minded brothers. Also on Sunday, when there is reading the whole day, this reading does not always bear fruit and the Abbot must see that the weaker brethren are occupied with some practical tasks (RB 48,22-23). Nor were these problems about which Benedict wrote specific to Italy. Two contemporaries, Ferreolus in Gaul and Fulgentius in Africa, attest to them in their own monasteries.

Conclusion: from the Fathers to the present

These realistic comments might encourage us, because they let us see that our modern difficulties with the *lectio divina* have their precedents in the past. The *lectio divina* is, and will always be, by its very nature, an austere task, a true spiritual sacrifice. The source of much generosity, it demands much generosity also.

Yet the failures here and there, as documented by the ancient writers, are outweighed by the massive success of the whole enterprise of the *lectio divina*. Saturated with the Bible, their writings show how much, without knowing it, the *lectio divina* has penetrated their lives. The *lectio* releases the imaginations of Christians to discover in the Old and New Testaments, on every page, the mystery of Christ in all its diversity – the historical life of Christ and the glory of his resurrection, his presence in the Church and in the interior life of our souls. Though it be a million miles away from our contemporary manner of scientific exegesis, the game of the *lectio* is still the same as it ever was (as experience shows): the instinctive attraction of the heart to Christ who dwells in it through faith.

Chapter 6

Lectio divina in Vatican II's Dogmatic Constitution *Dei Verbum*

Salvatore A. Panimolle

The Second Vatican Council's Dogmatic Constitution on Divine Revelation contains rich and stimulating doctrine upon how to read the Bible in such a way that it touches our life and gives us wisdom. The document also has ideas that are fruitful for the *lectio divina* today. It has important suggestions about how the Church feeds upon the divine nourishment of the Word and about the goal of this religious reading "in the Spirit": to establish a dialogue of love between our heavenly Father and his far-off children, pilgrims on earth. In fact the document does not present Holy Scripture only as the supreme rule of faith for the Christian community but also as the mirror of the community's life. Scripture is seen as the supreme Word of the Lord that must be the community's inspiration and the daily bread that sustains it.

1. *From listening to the Word to its contemplation*

Dei Verbum emphasizes on the vital role of devotional reading of the Bible for the whole Church in its pilgrimage towards its heavenly home. The Word is the food that supports the community of believers, which is nourished by this food in all the stages of its life, right up to the point of contemplating God and his marvellous acts in salvation. Listening to Scripture with devotion is the oil that feeds the lamp of faith. Indeed, it increases the flame of the lamp so that it makes the heart burn in ecstatic admiration for the

81

incredible love of our heavenly Father and of his Son, as revealed in the history of salvation and recorded in the Bible. In the same way that the hearts of the disciples on the Emmaus road burned within them while they listened to the risen Jesus explaining the Scriptures (Lk 24:32), the Church experiences a communion of charity with God and with its heavenly Spouse. The Church is thus ever more profoundly immersed in the Word; it reaches the heights of the purest contemplation. All the people of God, then, must constantly practise the *lectio divina*, so that they can have a deep experience of the life of love with the Father through the Son and in the Holy Spirit.

a) *The listening Church*

In its final version, the Council's document on Divine Revelation opens with an expression that shows the Church's hierarchy, met together in the holy Synod, in an attitude of reverence, humbly listening to the Word (*Dei verbum religiose audiens*). That is how the community of believers must present itself before its God who manifests himself. As Mary, Martha's sister, listened to the Lord while she sat at his feet (Lk 10:38ff), so the Church finds itself always listening to the Word, in order to proclaim the message of life to all the world and co-operate in its salvation (DV 1).

It is interesting to emphasize that in the preface to the Constitution the verb "listening" is one of the principal thematic words. Indeed it occurs three times (at the beginning, middle and end), so that it encapsulates the entire passage:

Dei verbum religiose *audiens*...
quod vidimus et *audivimus*...
mundus universus *audiendo* credat.

The Council is like the apostle who was an eye-witness of the saving ministry of Christ and who proclaimed what he had "seen and heard" of the Word of life (1 Jn 1:1.3). It listens to the divine words and announces them to the whole of humanity, so that by hearing they may believe, believing they may hope, and hoping they may love. Hence, in response to its proclamation of the Gospel, the Church looks to the world for an attitude of listening to the very same Word (DV 1).

This listening is put into practice in obedience to the faith that God reveals, trusting oneself fully to him and freely giving him the submission of one's intellect and will (DV 5). It is, therefore, a human assent to divine revelation by means of which people take the Word and make it their own, progressively interiorizing and assimilating it.

The attitude of listening with devotion is not reserved for the simple faithful and the incredulous, but it must also characterize the Teaching Office of the Church. For the Magisterium is not placed above the Word of God but is at its service. In fact the Magisterium must teach only what has been handed down, *listening to it devoutly*, guarding it scrupulously, and faithfully explaining it by divine commission and with the help of the Holy Spirit (DV 10). The expression "listening to it devoutly" (*pie audit*) in this passage recalls the initial expression of "listening... with reverence" (*religiose audiens*) (DV 1). They both refer to the hierarchy. The teachers of the faith must also live in an attitude of constant listening to the Word, subjecting themselves to its judgement, letting themselves be enlightened by it and, together with all the faithful, nourishing themselves continuously on this divine food (cf. DV 25).

b) *Contemplation by means of the Word*

Holy Scripture and sacred Tradition are the mirrors in which the pilgrim Church on earth *contemplates God* till it sees him fully in glory. Listening to the Word, therefore, the community of believers contemplates the one who is at its origin and from whom it receives everything (DV 7). The mirror of divine revelation reflects its author in a true way, even though it does not show him in his perfect features. For the Church's earthly pilgrimage is carried out in faith and is a preparation for the vision to come at the end of its exodus, in its heavenly home.

The same theme in the New Testament can be found in the Letter of James. Unfortunately, however, the Council's text does not mention the passage, even in a footnote. The passage is the famous one of James 1:22ff, which the remaining paragraphs of *Dei Verbum* do not consider either. In this passage James, the servant of God and of the Lord Jesus Christ, presents Scripture as a mirror, in which the person who hears the Word gazes upon his own face. In this place too the Bible is regarded as an instrument of contemplation, although what is seen is not God but the person who looks at himself. Nonetheless, it would seem to be an important notion that the Word offers sufficient light to reflect, as in a mirror, the true outline of a person, who in DV 7 is God.

Actually, the whole biblical tradition presents the Word of God as light: "Thy word is a lamp to my feet and a light to my path" (Ps 119:105; cf. Prov 6:23; Bar 3:14; Jn 1:4f; 1 Jn 2:8 etc.). This divine light does not merely clear away the shadows of the world and of humanity. It reveals and manifests its author. Hence to contemplate the face of God, even if more in the mystery of faith than in full vision (cf. 1 Cor 13:12), the Church's only true means is through the Word.

The way to such contemplation is through meditation or wisdom-filled study of or devotional listening to divine revelation, which is contained in Holy Scripture or sacred Tradition (DV 7).

Plunging into such light, the Church shines bright and cooperates in clearing away the shadows of the world, by announcing the word of Jesus, the light of all nations (*Lumen gentium*). This is how the Dogmatic Constitution on the Church begins:

> Christ is the light of all nations. Hence this most sacred Synod, which has been gathered in the Holy Spirit, eagerly desires to shed on all men that radiance of his which brightens the countenance of the Church. This it will do by proclaiming the gospel to every creature (LG 1).

The community of believers is transformed and given splendour by contemplating the Son of God made flesh (cf. Jn 1:14), so that it can shine this light upon the whole world. A comparison can be made with an object of iron. It is cold by nature but becomes white-hot if it is left for long in a powerful flame and almost changes its own qualities by acquiring those of the fire. In a similar fashion the Church, if it lets itself be penetrated profoundly by the light of the Word through long contemplation, loses its shadows, its coldness and its sinfulness. It becomes transformed, all splendid and beautiful, purified by its Spouse (cf. Eph 5:26f).

2. *The dialogue of love*

In fact, in the profound listening to the Word through devotional reading of the Bible, in other words through the *lectio divina*, the Church carries on a beatifying and transformative dialogue with its God and its beloved Spouse. The true conversation of love between the heavenly Father and his children who are far from home comes about through contact with his Word, reverently read or listened to profoundly. In this way, the community of believers receives the message of life and listens to the voice of God, letting itself be guided by his Spirit. It admires and contemplates the wonders of love recorded in the history of salvation and it responds in a filial manner to the Word which summons and invites it to an ever deeper acceptance and consistency in faith.

a) *God dwells as a friend with the human race*

After the preface, the first chapter of *Dei Verbum* begins by presenting divine revelation as an instrument that divinizes human beings and gives them the experience of a deep, intimate and friendly communion with God (DV 2). Indeed, moved by his goodness and wisdom, he has been pleased to make himself known to his human creation, revealing to it his plan of salvation (cf. Eph 1:9). In this divine plan human beings, by means of the Word made flesh, have access to the Father in the Holy Spirit, and they become partakers of the divine nature (cf. 2 Pt 1:4). They are introduced therefore into communion with the Blessed Trinity, ceasing to be strangers but becoming members of the family of God (Eph 2:18ff).

This is the way in which the Father, revealing the economy of salvation which has its centre and perfect mediator in Christ (Eph 1:9ff), communicates the divine life to the human race. Humanity becomes his friend and his child, and he dwells amiably with it. He is urged on by the fire of his charity. And so when he makes himself known, God transforms people and makes them his "partners". He raises them up to the dignity of friends and speaks with them and lives among them like a friend (DV 2). Believers, therefore, repeat the experience that Moses had when he spoke to God face to face (Ex 33:11). God, in revealing himself, communicated his Wisdom to the people. Consequently, Wisdom has appeared upon the earth and has lived among men (Bar 3:37f), because it has been made flesh in the Son of God (Jn 1:14). He, who was the perfect revelation in person (Jn 1:17, 14:6), dwelt together with his disciples, considering them no longer as servants but as friends, to whom he made known all that he had heard and seen of the Father (Jn 15:14f).

b) *The incarnate Word, instrument of perfect dialogue*

God, having spoken at various times through the prophets in the Old Testament, spoke his final word in the Son, the heir to the universe and the mediator of creation (Heb 1:1f). Perfect dialogue between the self-revealing God and humanity comes about in and through the incarnate Word. For he is in fact the definitive Word that the Father says to the world (Jn 1:1f). He was sent upon earth to give light to the human race and to dwell with it, so that he could make known the innermost life of God (DV 4). The fourth evangelist presents the Son of God to us particularly in this perspective: he not only speaks the words of God (Jn 3:34), giving witness to the divine realities that he sees and hears continuously (Jn 3:11.32, 18:37), but he is full of grace and truth (Jn 1:14). Therefore, the gift of the perfect revelation came about by means of him, the only Son of the Father (Jn 1:17f); indeed, it is identified with him (Jn 14:6).

True and perfect dialogue between God and man thus happens in the God-man, Jesus Christ, the eschatological bringer of revelation. In him the Father speaks to human beings and they are enabled to reply to the divine invitation, opening up a conversation with the Father, who is seen and heard in the Word made flesh (Jn 14:9ff).

With this Word, recorded in the Gospel, God continues to speak uninterruptedly with the bride of his Son, and the conversation of love between the heavenly Father and the children of the Church is not broken off by Jesus' ascension. It is carried on by means of the proclamation of the Christian Good News (DV 8). The *lectio divina* of the Gospel, consequently, is a privileged moment in making the dialogue between God and the disciples of his Son come about in fact.

c) *The heavenly Father talks with his children in Holy Scripture*

The last chapter of *Dei Verbum* makes even more explicit that devotional reading of the Word is a conversation. Scripture gives voice to the Holy Spirit in the words of the prophets and the apostles, indeed "in the sacred books, the Father who is in heaven meets his children with great love (*peramanter*) and speaks with them" (DV 21).

God's authentic dialogue with his Church takes place when the Church listens to the Word. In the *lectio divina*, whether in the liturgy or in private, the heavenly Father makes his message heard and his family replies with faith and acts of thanksgiving, with supplication and weeping. Thus a conversation between persons who love one another is begun, even though it cannot be seen as quite the same for both sides, because the initiative is always and only God's. It is he who speaks, who addresses himself to the Church, who makes known his immense love. It is he who first loved us (cf. 1 Jn 4:10), and who invites us to enter into communion with him.

The role of believers in this dialogue is principally one of listening, of welcoming the Word, of praising the love and wisdom of the Father, of confessing their own infidelities, of imploring divine forgiveness.

3. *The action of the Spirit*

So far as faith is concerned, the Holy Spirit plays an extremely important role in God's loving dialogue with the Church by means of his Word. This role goes from the birth of faith to its becoming mature through facilitating the deeper grasp of revelation and the interiorization of truth.

a) *In the process of faith*

Dei Verbum teaches first of all that the divinization of the human being comes about by means of the Word incarnate. It is this divinization that makes the life of communion possible and means that we can converse with the Father in listening to the Word of Scripture. But it comes about in the Holy Spirit (DV 2). The third Person of the Trinity is therefore the spiritual atmosphere in which God's "partner" is raised to the supernatural sphere. He is the spiritual atmosphere in which human beings enter into God's family, so that they become children of God and can listen to and call upon God as Father. A similar teaching is put forward in Jesus' conversation with Nicodemus: only in the Holy Spirit and by means of him is it possible to be born to the supernatural life or to become children of God (Jn 3:3ff), which is achieved through believing in the name of the Father's only

Son (Jn 1:12f). Hence not only the divinization of the human creature but consequently also dialoguing with God during the reverent reading of the Bible can only come about through the action of the Holy Spirit who gives birth to faith and revives it.

The process of adhering to divine revelation comes about by the power of the Holy Spirit, that is, from when faith is born to the deepening of understanding or its perfecting. In effect the human being believes in God, who makes himself known, with the help of grace and of the Holy Spirit, who moves the heart and turns it to God, who opens the eyes of the mind and gives to all the willingness to assent and believe in the truth. Therefore the initial act of faith comes about under the determining action of the Holy Spirit (DV 5).

The outpouring of the Spirit in the deeper understanding of Christian revelation made itself felt strongly at the beginning, when the apostles and the sacred writers recorded what they had learnt from Christ and what had been suggested to them by the Holy Spirit (DV 7). Therefore, the action of the Spirit was decisive not only in the final moment, when the announcement of salvation was proclaimed (cf. DV 9,11,18,20), but also in the process of expanding upon and penetrating into the words and acts of Christ. The apostles, in fact, did not simply proclaim and transmit what they had seen and heard in their life of communion with the Lord Jesus, which spanned from the moment of their calling to the ascension. They also passed on what they had learnt through the suggestions of the Spirit: *a Spiritu sancto suggerente didicerant* (DV 7).

The action of the Spirit made itself powerfully felt upon the apostles and the prophets in the manifestation of the saving mystery centred around the Word of God, from his incarnation, his exaltation in the resurrection and ascension into heaven (DV 17). That this doctrine was the inspiration of Ephesians 3:4f would seem to be obvious. Here the writer teaches that the sacrament (*mysterion*) of Christ was revealed only now to his holy apostles and prophets in the

Spirit. The Dogmatic Constitution, however, states clearly that the outpouring of the Holy Spirit upon these privileged persons was not limited to the initial phase of the manifestation of the mystery of salvation, but it continued also in their missionary activity:

> So that they might preach the Gospel, stir up faith in Jesus, Christ and Lord, and gather the Church together (DV 17).

As a consequence, the whole process of the birth of the Christian community took place under the action of the Spirit who sustained and guided the witness of the apostles, making it fruitful for winning people over to the message of the Gospel.

Furthermore, the outpouring of the Spirit was decisive in the growing understanding and the development of the Christian message of salvation in the apostles' minds and hearts. Indeed, after the Lord's ascension, they handed on what Jesus had said and done, together with the full comprehension they had gained from the events of Christ's life and the light of the Spirit of truth (DV 19). Thus it was not just the resurrection of Jesus that showed the events of his earthly life in a new perspective, but the Holy Spirit exercising a decisive influence in the deepening grasp of the message and person of the Lord Jesus. Now, how did such a better and clearer comprehension of the sacrament that was Christ come about, if not through meditating upon his acts and his words? And in what does the *lectio divina* essentially consist, if not in a reverent listening to the Gospel and Holy Scripture?

b) *In the growing understanding of revelation*

Hence the deeper comprehension (*intelligentia*) of the divine word is the work of the Holy Spirit:

> To bring about an ever deeper understanding of revelation, the same Holy Spirit constantly brings faith to completion by his gifts (DV 5).

90

This affirmation is significant for our specific concern because it suggests that true *lectio divina* is carried out with the help of the Holy Spirit, or in other words, putting oneself under the influence of God. Obviously this growing in the understanding of revelation has to do with the whole life of the Church and the complex action of penetrating and explaining the Word. But in this process, it is necessary to reserve an important place for devotional reading of the Bible, in which both individuals and communities of the faithful really attempt to enter into the hidden mysteries of divine revelation.

In reality such a process of deepening, and of broadening and clarifying, the understanding of revelation is not limited only to the initial phase. It carries on throughout the history of the Church. The Constitution teaches that the apostolic tradition, or the message of salvation passed on by the apostles to the Christian community, progresses and develops (*proficit*) in the Church by the help of the Holy Spirit:

> For there is a growth in the understanding of the realities and words which have been handed down. This happens through the contemplation and study made by believers, who treasure these things in their hearts... through the intimate understanding of spiritual things they experience (DV 8).

Such statements deserve special attention, because they clearly allude to the *lectio divina*. What does one actually do during the devotional reading of the Word if not study, meditate and contemplate the divine revelation handed down from the apostles and recorded in writing? In the above passage there is explicit mention of Luke 2:19.51, which is where the mother of Jesus is described as the first believer who kept in her heart all the words about her son or said by him. Mary, therefore, is the model of the Church that meditates upon and deepens its understanding of the Word.

It is important to stress that such deeper understanding or growth of revelation occurs in a very special way during the *lectio divina*, namely, at the time when the community of believers puts itself under the guidance of the Holy Spirit in order to hear, study and contemplate the Word handed down by the apostles. This provides good conditions for the Church's ceaseless journey towards the fullness of truth (DV 8).

But the Holy Spirit does not only make the living voice of the Gospel resound in the Church. He also leads individuals into the whole truth. Thus the Word of Christ becomes a living reality and a source of life by means of the Spirit, as Jesus had taught in the face of the disbelief of many of his disciples. "It is the spirit that gives life, the flesh is of no avail; the words that I have spoken to you are spirit and life" (Jn 6:63).

Lighting the flame of faith in the individual heart, the Holy Spirit makes a person accept the Gospel, which is seen as the word of life. And the Spirit guides the disciples of Christ to the fullness of truth, in other words, to the revelation given by the Word made flesh (DV 8). Even though *Dei Verbum* does not have here any reference to the Fourth Gospel, the echo of John 16:13 is very strong. To show this all that is needed is to compare two passages:

> The Spirit of truth *will guide you into all the truth* (Jn 16:13);
> The Holy Spirit... *leads unto all truth those who believe* (DV 8).

The specific function, then, of the Spirit in relation to revelation is to lead the Church into the heart of the mystery of Christ, guiding it towards the fullness of truth, seen as the manifestation of the love of the Father in his Son Jesus Christ, the truth in person (Jn 14:6).

In the final passage of chapter V, the Dogmatic Constitution teaches this same doctrine of the Holy Spirit's function in leading the disciples of Jesus into the fullness of revelation. At this point John 16:13 is cited: "For the Lord Jesus... sent to them as *Paraclete the Spirit* who would *lead them into the fullness of truth* (DV 20).

92

For our purposes it is well worth looking at the relationship between the *lectio divina* and the action of the Holy Spirit. In fact, in the Constitution we find interesting hints or suggestions about a profound and devout listening to the Word.

Towards the end of chapter II, the document teaches that the Magisterium's service to revelation comes into play when the Word is listened to with devotion (*pie audit*), and is scrupulously guarded and faithfully explained with the help of the Holy Spirit (DV 10). This is clearly not true only for the pastors and teachers of the Christian people, but also all the other faithful: the devout hearing of the Word can only come about through the outpouring of the Spirit.

But "Holy Scripture must be read and interpreted according to the same Spirit by whom it was written": *eodem Spiritu quo est etiam legenda et interpretanda* (DV 12). This sentence, added to the final version of the document, is inspired by the Encyclical *Spiritus Paraclitus* of Benedict XV. The Encyclical contains an expression of St Jerome in his commentary on St Paul's Letter to the Galatians. We print it, in context, below:

> Whoever tries to understand the Scriptures in a sense different from that inspired by the Spirit who is its author, even though such a person may not in fact be away from the Church, nevertheless may be counted a heretic. For he is born of the flesh, hence opts for the worst.

The Encyclical explains that this great Catholic exegete was well aware of the need for the intervention of the Spirit of God for a correct exposition of the Holy Scriptures. Scripture must be read and understood according to the meaning of the Holy Spirit who is besought in personal prayer, united to that of one's friends. Hence both the *lectio divina* and a profound exegesis of the Bible must begin with calling upon the Lord to obtain the light of the Paraclete.

Dei Verbum makes explicit here that reading and exegesis of the Word "in the Spirit" is greatly helped by the hermeneutic principle we could call of "comprehensiveness". This is used when a text is understood and explained in the light of the content and unity of the whole of Scripture, bearing in mind the living tradition of the whole Church and the harmony that exists between elements of the faith (DV 12). For while the Bible was written by numerous human authors, it has a single divine author: the Holy Spirit who, as we have already seen, does not only inspire the sacred writers; he also helps and guides the community of believers in the process of growth and deeper understanding of the Word. The Spirit of God therefore is the principle of unity for Holy Scripture and for its development in the life of the Church. Consequently, true *lectio divina* and a deep "spiritual" exposition of the Bible will shed light on the pages that are studied and considered. Not only is this done by making use of parallel passages, but it is done by putting them under the searchlight of revelation taken in its comprehensiveness.

In fact, the Scriptures communicate the Word of God himself and in the expressions of the prophets and apostles they give voice to the Holy Spirit (DV 21). Therefore the Spirit speaks to the Church and to individual believers, when Scripture is read in the assembly of the people of God. During the liturgy and in the *lectio divina*, whether personally or in the community, the faithful hear the voice of the Spirit, because they believe that the Bible is not mere human words, but the Word that the Spirit says to the Christian communities and to individual members (cf. Rev 2:7.11.17.29). Indeed, Scripture may and should be seen as the letter that the heavenly Father sends to his exiled children, pilgrims on this earth, with whom he speaks through the Holy Spirit (DV 21).

With this hearing of the Word which becomes concrete in the liturgical assembly and in private *lectio divina*, the bride of the Word made flesh is taught by the Holy Spirit and strives for a grasp (*intelligentia*) of Holy Scripture that is deeper every day. Consequently, the ever deeper penetration of the Word, the development in understanding as its contents are made clear, its beneficial effects upon believers are greatly aided by devotional reading of the Bible.

The Church improves its grasp not only of speculative knowledge of Scripture, but also, and above all, of its value in life and its meaning for salvation, and it nourishes its children with the divine food of the Word (DV 23). The *lectio divina* is one of the privileged moments of this spiritual nourishment. Thus it contributes greatly to the ever deeper understanding and enrichment of divine revelation.

4. *The stages of the* lectio divina

Dei Verbum does not simply put into relief the importance of devotional reading and its value for life. It also illustrates the various elements of a true and effective listening to Holy Scripture. Obviously, the document does not describe the four traditional stages in an organic fashion. They are, however, all present, up to and including the sublime moment of the contemplation of God. In the preceding pages we have already shown some of these elements. In these final paragraphs we wish to put the four stages into focus by presenting them systematically.

a) *Devotional reading*

The first stage of the *lectio divina* is the reverent and devout listening to the Word. One reads sacred Scripture with faith and one re-reads it carefully, in order to feed upon this divine food. We have already been able to see the clarity and pre-eminence of listening to revelation devoutly in the Dogmatic Constitution (DV 10).

The Word of God, together with the eucharistic body of Christ, is presented first of all as the heavenly bread that Mother Church offers to her children. It is divine food that nourishes the faithful and feeds the Christian religion, as a pure and everlasting source of spiritual life (DV 21). Such

95

nourishment comes with an understanding and devout reading of the Word. As a result, the Council was at pains to recommend accurate and faithful translations of the Scriptures into modern languages, so that the faithful may feed upon this divine bread (DV 22,25).

The bride of the Word made flesh wishes constantly to nourish her children with the divine words (DV 23). The Dogmatic Constitution, consequently, in the first place exhorts preachers and catechists to hold fast to a diligent sacred reading (*lectione sacra*) of the Bible, so that they do not run the risk of being empty proclaimers, because they do not hear the Word within themselves (DV 25). In this passage, then, we find almost an equivalence between the *lectio divina* and the listening to the Word. In this way it is strongly suggested that devotional reading of the Bible consists in an attentive and profound listening.

Not only the ministers of the Word, however, but also the religious and all the faithful ought to hold fast to acquiring "the surpassing worth of knowing Christ Jesus" (Phil 3:8) through a constant and unwearied reading of the Bible:

> This sacred Synod earnestly and specifically urges all the Christian faithful too, especially religious, to learn by frequent reading of the divine Scriptures the "excelling knowledge of Jesus Christ" (Phil 3:8). "For ignorance of the Scriptures is ignorance of Christ" (DV 25).

If, therefore, knowledge of the Lord Jesus is proportional to knowledge of the Bible, it would seem to be quite logical for the Council to exhort people to become familiar with the sacred text not just during liturgical celebrations, but also through the *lectio divina* called *pia lectio*. In fact, the document is concerned that the children of the Church should become full of the spirit of the Scriptures by means of a continuous contact with them (DV 25).

The Council looks for abundant fruits of salvation from this practice of devotional reading of the Bible: namely, the spread and the glorification of the Word, an ever greater acceptance of the treasure of revelation in the hearts of humanity and a new surge in the spiritual life (DV 26). The frequent exercise of the *lectio divina* seems therefore to be a source of grace not only for the Church but also for the whole world, given the missionary significance of 2 Thessalonians 3:1.

Hence the constant and profound hearing of the Word produces health-giving effects for all: for believers, in that it feeds and revives their commitment to Christ; for all other people, because it prepares for their evangelization.

b) *Meditation and study*

The *lectio divina*, however, includes also meditation and serious study, in order to grasp the true meaning of the Word and not to run the risk of misunderstanding the divine message. The Dogmatic Constitution illustrates this necessary stage of devotional reading of the Bible as well.

Speaking of the development and deeper understanding of revelation, the document teaches that this growth is favoured in a special way by the contemplation and study of believers, who imitate the behaviour of the Virgin Mary (DV 8). This reference to the example of the mother of the Lord suggests that the *lectio divina* has a moment of reflection or meditation (cf. Lk 2:19.51). The ancient monastic Fathers called this *ruminatio*, to indicate the act of tasting, of relishing the Word.

But this stage in the devotional reading of the Bible requires an accurate study of the sacred texts, or at least knowledge of the scholarly conclusions of professional exegetes, and using good (if sober) introductions to individual books as well as explanatory comments upon the most difficult passages (DV 25). For this reason it is necessary to be aware of the main literary genres of the various parts that make up Holy Scripture (DV 12).

Biblical scholars are encouraged to carry on their research in particular in a pastoral perspective. By doing so, they can help the ministers of the Word to share out the divine bread in a health-giving manner (DV 23,24) and help the formation of the Church's judgement upon various problems of Christian ethics and faith (DV 24). But priests, deacons and catechists are also exhorted to study the Scripture: *assidua lectione sacra atque exquisito studio* in order to discover and communicate the tremendous riches of the Word (DV 25). Such devotional reading and serious study of the Bible also contributes to the Church's missionary expansion, apart from its spiritual growth (DV 26).

c) *Prayer*

The Dogmatic Constitution does not pass over the third stage of the *lectio divina*: prayer. Indeed, towards the end of the document we find the following exhortation, that all the faithful ought to

> ...remember that prayer should accompany the reading of sacred Scripture, so that God and man may talk together; for "we speak to him when we pray; we hear him when we read the divine sayings" (DV 25).

The importance of prayer in the *lectio divina* is put into light here, and it is shown as a dialogue of love with the heavenly Father. Listening to the Word which gives voice to the Spirit (DV 21), the believer replies by praising and blessing the Lord, imploring mercy for his own and all the world's infidelities, calling for the help of grace to live out the message of the divine. In this way a profound dialogue begins and develops between the Father who utters his true word and his children who welcome the divine message with faith. It is a dialogue without illusions and fantasies, and the acceptance of the divine message is accompanied by prayer (DV 25).

In fact, "the Father who is in heaven meets his children with great love (*peramanter*) and speaks with them" (DV 21). As a result, the *lectio divina* is a real conversation in which God who speaks reveals his love and the human being who replies with quiet acceptance shows his faith, confesses the wonders worked by the Lord, recognizes his own sin and pleads with this good and merciful Father.

God, in this manner, speaks with the bride of his beloved Son, and the Holy Spirit makes the living voice of the Gospel heard in the Church and through it heard in all the world (DV 8). The community of believers responds to the Word, transforming their listening into prayer. This, then, opens up the dialogue in faith and love between the heavenly Father and his children which is the result of the *lectio divina* (DV 25).

d) *Contemplation*

As we suggested above, *Dei Verbum* does not ignore the final stage of a profound and devout hearing of the Word: the contemplation of God and his marvellous works in salvation. As it speaks about the handing down of revelation, the document presents Tradition and Scripture as "like a mirror in which the pilgrim Church on earth *looks at* God" (DV 7). Obviously, this is a contemplation in faith and not the full vision, face to face, that is reserved for the end of time in the heavenly homeland (cf. 1 Jn 3:2).

Such contemplation of the Word does not constitute only the moment of joy in the meeting of the bride with her Spouse, Christ. It is also the normal instrument for the development of revelation (DV 8).

The Church meditating and contemplating the words and divine events passed down to her, day by day deepens its comprehension of them and of their content. Just as the mother of Jesus reflected for a long time upon the actions and the words regarding her Son (cf. Lk 2:19.51), the faithful study, contemplate and have a profound experience of the Christian mystery, and that facilitates the growth of what is given by revelation (DV 8).

Contemplation is the summit of the dialogue of love between the heavenly Father and the faithful, when they feed upon the nourishing food of the Word and taste the sweetness of this pure and everlasting source of spiritual life by means of the *lectio divina* (DV 21).

Conclusion: calling upon the Holy Spirit in the lectio divina

At the end of our reflections, we will conclude by summarizing what we have said about the Holy Spirit in the devout listening to the Word. We have been able to see the determining role of the Spirit's action for a reading of the Bible that is not merely technical or profane. Now we wish to focus upon what the Dogmatic Constitution puts forward insofar as it seems to be important for a true and living *lectio divina*: that is, prayer to the Spirit of the Lord that he might open our minds and guide our hearts as we listen to the Word.

He, indeed, is the one divine author of the whole of Scripture, and therefore he alone can unveil its secret mysteries, lead us into all truth (Jn 16:13), sound the unfathomable depths of revelation, and make us discover the hidden treasures of the divine plan of salvation.

Paul lifts up a hymn to this sublime plan of salvation, so shocking to the human mind: "O depth of the riches and wisdom and knowledge of God! How unsearchable are his judgements and inscrutable his ways!" (Rom 11:13). But he teaches that these depths are sounded only by the Spirit of the Lord and he makes them known to us:

God has revealed to us [what no eye has seen, nor ear heard] through the Spirit. For the Spirit searches everything, even the depths of God (1 Cor 2:10).

Dei Verbum cites Benedict XV's Encyclical *Spiritus Paraclitus*, saying that

Holy Scripture must be read and interpreted according to the same Spirit by whom it was written (DV 12).

In doing so, it certainly refers to St Jerome's doctrine, which is actually cited in the footnote. When this great master of exegesis uses a similar expression, he explains that a "spiritual" reading of the Bible is possible only through prayer to the Paraclete, and not just at its beginning but also during it. We have illustrated this theme above. It is clear then: to transform the listening to the Word into authentic *lectio divina* it is necessary to put oneself under the guidance of the one who is Scripture's principal author, the one who thought of it, brought it into existence and made it known, and thus knows its secrets, its hidden richness and its divine depths.

For this reason, the document rightly stresses that in the dialogue of faith and love between the heavenly Father and the bride of his Son, the Holy Spirit makes the living voice of the Gospel ring out in the Church and in the whole world, as well as leading believers to the fullness of truth (DV 8). In other words, he helps them to penetrate the secret wonders of the love of God, recorded in the book that contains his Word.

In fact, the Spirit of the Lord sets faith alight in the human heart, and he increasingly gives new life to this divine flame. With this same light, the believer sees the richness hidden in Holy Scripture better and is able to engage in a true *lectio divina* which is transformed into a profound and real conversation with the heavenly Father.

Chapter 7

The *lectio divina* in pastoral life

Cadinal Carlo-Maria Martini

1. *Scripture and the pastoral life*

In our time the gap between faith and daily living is causing grave difficulties to developing the mission of the Church. The pastoral life of the Church is badly in need of a deep renewal. Furthermore, faith must be understood as a dynamic process enabling the faithful to proclaim in word and deed the paschal mystery of Christ. Faith grows through listening to the Word of God. The Vatican Council puts it this way:

> God, who spoke of old, uninterruptedly converses with the Bride of his beloved Son; and the Holy Spirit, through whom the living voice of the gospel resounds in the Church, and through her, in the world, leads unto all truth those who believe and makes the word of Christ dwell abundantly in them (DV 8).

Nor is that all; the Word of God "grows". In the Acts of the Apostles (6:7) we read: "And the Word of God increased; and the number of the disciples multiplied greatly in Jerusalem." It is an interesting fact that Luke uses the same word *auxánô* to describe Jesus growing up in Nazareth and the Word growing through the proclamation of the Apostles. The Word of God grows quite simply because it is "alive" and because it is addressed to men and women who must live and grow because of it.

The realization of what is happening in the transformation of a community under the Word's influence is an amazing surprise. People who remain foreigners to the Word remain apathetic, silent and unresponsive to what they are hearing. They do not grow in communion with the mystery and are incapable of expressing the faith in their lives.

St Gregory the Great used to say that the Bible was given to everyone, though not everyone could understand everything in it. No one individual could ever exhaust the religious experience of the whole People of God. And so the challenge comes down to every generation; it is the Word that arouses a living faith. Going around my diocese as a bishop I am constantly aware of the need among people for the Word of God. It is expressed in their desire to go together on the journey of faith, and in the practical possibility of going on this journey.

Yet there still remains a great deal of ignorance of the Scriptures among our people, and even among the best educated. Often I am asked the most elementary of questions by people which reveal that they have no clear idea of the constitution of the Bible, its organization and structure, the relationship between the "Gospel" and the "Bible", etc. In fact, the Bible has not formed the solid, substantial diet for the faith and devotion of the faithful for a long time. That is why the Second Vatican Council (DV 6) insisted that all the faithful have access to the Scriptures.

When this happens, *contact* with the Word brings about surprising life. It is an experience that all can have, ordinary people and the young as well. And I, who have been reading the Scriptures for about forty years, still find something new and enriching every day, something that amazes me, giving me the shock of an understanding and a new feeling that creates a deeper awareness of human values and that puts me in touch with the values of God himself.

2. *The* lectio divina *and the school of the Word*

It is apparent then that access to the Scriptures is all important for the faithful. Today more than ever Scripture can open up the sense of mystery in our lives, an awareness of the infinite, a desire to reach out towards God. One way of developing our pastoral life is a Bible School or what I call

"The School of the Word". In Milan over the past five years I have gathered young people together on the first Thursday of the month at the Cathedral. We adopt that gradual approach so loved by the Fathers, and which is similar to the one used by the rabbis, known as the *lectio divina*. In the Jewish world the Scriptures were taught in schools in a very simple and down-to-earth way, though there are certain basic pedagogical and philological rules which follow a precise progression. Were this not the case the exercise could end up being very boring and dry, even counterproductive. Here, in brief, are the principles for teaching the *lectio divina* and the method.

a) *The unity of Scripture*

It is important to help people understand that though the Bible is composed of many books there is a fundamental unity underlying it all. Every page spells out the grand design of God to save mankind. If Christians do not understand this principle, their efforts to read Scripture come to nothing: perhaps they begin at the Book of Genesis and find it interesting, then they carry on, but when they get to the Book of Numbers, they are stuck and go no further. Only by trying to draw back to unity the mystery of every Bible page, can all the pages then speak.

b) *Scripture's humanity or its way of dealing with real life*

Scripture speaks to each one of us. It captures the most precious movements of the human heart, our unease, our suffering, our dreams, our desires. We read about ourselves when we read the Bible; humanity as it always is, humanity that speaks of itself and of its hope and of its wretchedness. By taking up simple examples of *lectio divina*, in our School of the Word, people discover in reading the sacred texts something about themselves, both as a person or as a community, without which we do not see ourselves as a whole.

c) *The unfolding of values*

Scripture holds up to us values that still today are continually unfolding into the future; they are dynamic not static values. From both the points of view of moral life and of intellectual stimulation, the Bible contains values that generate a desire to go beyond oneself, making us feel that humanity is on a journey. It intersects with human life, a movement from life to the Word and returning from the Word to life. Men and women come to the Bible bearing their human dignity, the burden of their freedom, their spiritual uncertainties, their intricacies, their stirrings of courage and of hope, their true but precarious victories in all areas of human existence. The pages of Scripture are studded with human situations made meaningful and redeemed by the Word of God: even the pages that document acts of cruelty, suffering, distress, sin, which throw into relief the process of conversion. We are thus strengthened to carry on and to pick up our daily burdens, going forward with new hope and renewed commitment.

d) *In Scripture there is the real presence of Jesus*

Whenever we read Scripture we are able to enter into real communion with Jesus. At first sight such an expression might seem surprising; it reminds us of the eucharistic presence. Yet Vatican II did not hesitate to use it. The risen Christ is present in his Scriptures. One has only to read and listen to the Scriptures to experience the truth of it (*Sacrosanctum Concilium*, 7).

e) *The method of* lectio divina

Since much has already been written about this we shall not dwell too long upon it. Suffice it to say that the Christian tradition has developed a programme for the *lectio divina*, comprising four elements: *lectio, meditatio, oratio* and *con-*

templatio. This fourfold sequence is the fruit of theological and anthropological reflection upon how the faithful apprehend the Word of God, assimilate and translate it into their daily living.

(i) *Lectio* – What is meant here is reading and re-reading the text. The important points are highlighted, the events, the words, the personalities involved, the emotions, the circumstances, the unfolding of the action. This careful exploration results in many surprising discoveries as we get to know the text.

(ii) *Meditatio* – The second step concentrates on the values implicit in a passage. What values underpin the actions, the words, the things, the feelings spoken of? We strive to grasp the central values, the specific message with reference to the story, the context and the situation.

The person seeking for his or her true self and searching for God recognizes the attitudes that underlie the pages he or she is pondering upon: joy, fear, hope, longing, expectation...

(iii) *Oratio* – Slowly the reader becomes caught up in the profound religious feelings that the text produces or suggests in the name of God; the values that *meditatio* discovered become reasons for praise, thanksgiving, supplication, petitions, asking forgiveness...

(iv) *Contemplatio* – There comes a point when this combination of emotion, reflection and prayer becomes focused on the mystery of Christ, the Son of God. This is the mystery on every page of Scripture, especially in the gospels, though, proportionally, in every part of the Bible.

3. *The* lectio divina *and daily living*

One might ask: does the *lectio divina* find its term in contemplation? At first sight it might appear to be the case but in fact the movement goes on.

The structure of our consciousness by which we progress

from thinking to acting is complex and fertile. It requires the dynamics of feelings, the evaluation of choices, the decision to deliberate. When we hear, for example, of someone who prays in order to act better, often what is meant is the request for strength to do what was decided before praying. But the Word of God, heard and accepted in faith, has the task of making Christ Jesus, the living Word of God, transform the human life of the Christian into himself. For Christians are called to become the word themselves, the sign of God's love and of communication with him.

Through the *lectio divina* the Christian must ask a question: how is my life, my action, my witness becoming a word of God, in the light of the definitive Word of God, Jesus Christ, present in Scripture? The *lectio*, then, struggles to bring the faith into the midst of our daily lives, holds us in the service of the kingdom of God and keeps our faith strong. It does so by means of three activities: *discretio, deliberatio* and *actio*.

(i) *Discretio* – By this we mean the Christian's capacity acquired by means of the Holy Spirit to know what is compatible with the Gospel and what is not. It is the ability to discern in any given historical moment what is best for oneself, for others, for the Church.

(ii) *Deliberatio* – This is the actual choosing of what is right in the light of the Gospel.

(iii) *Actio* – This is the doing of what has been decided. Only thus does action become spiritual, *secundum Deum*, a practical way of thinking and operating born in the Christian and guided by the Holy Spirit. Obviously, there will be many different educational approaches.

4. *Some concrete pastoral suggestions about the* lectio divina

It is indispensable for Christians to have practical means of submitting themselves to the Word of God and of comparing their lives with it in a realistic way. The *lectio divina* is one of these means, and people can learn how to do it through the School of the Word. Christians, in this way, slowly learn how to detect, in the ambiguity of history, the signs and the presence of the Spirit in the midst of his people and of the community.

The *lectio divina* is not restricted to a few highly committed people or to special prayer groups. In the present secular world, without it we will cease to be true Christians. The world today is crying out for people who are contemplative, alert, critical, courageous. At times the world will require new and unheard-of choices. And it will require care and emphasis on things that do not come from mere habit nor from public opinion, but rather from listening to the Word of the Lord and from the perception of the mysterious action of the Holy Spirit in the heart.

A few suggestions for the lectio divina

a) Before beginning any Parish Council Meeting or Catholic Action Group pause for a moment's *lectio divina*: a short reading from Scripture, a short silence, a sharing of what the Spirit has brought to mind for each person in the period of silence and then a moment of prayer of praise. Where people are able to meditate together, to contemplate together, they are more able to think about practical issues. The time spent apparently to the detriment of discussion will greatly benefit our pastoral activities.

b) Introduce practices of a meditative character that link with what is celebrated in the liturgy. We can gradually accustom our people to familiarize themselves with the four steps of the *lectio divina*. This can be led by the clergy or a small group of trained people beginning with the liturgical texts of the Sunday liturgy. Those who now recite Lauds either in the parish or alone could be encouraged to spend just three or four minutes on a very brief *lectio divina*.

c) Families could gather together once a week to pray and come to learn the *lectio divina*. In a little book, written in 1984 entitled *Teach us to pray as a family*, I invited all families in the Milan area to pray a psalm together over the Christmas period. I explained very simply how one could pray over a page of the Gospel, using the method of the *lectio divina*.

d) Each time an important event takes place in our lives, be it joyful or sad, start to interpret it with a reading from the Old or the New Testament. When we examine our consciences or when we prepare ourselves for sacramental reconciliation, we can try to transform the examination of our sins into a *lectio divina*. We put ourselves before a page of the Bible (we might take the Sunday readings or a verse of one of the psalms) to set a true standard by which to judge ourselves and how loving we have been.

e) Anyone who wants to grow into maturity of faith has to become used to practising a daily *lectio divina*. On one day we might concentrate on the *lectio*; another day we might dwell on the *meditatio* or the *contemplatio*. What is vital, however, is that every day there should be something that flows from the *lectio*.

Conclusion

I have simply offered these few suggestions in the certainty that among the hopes for pastoral renewal envisaged by the Church in the Vatican Council can be numbered the rediscovery and the spread of the *lectio divina* at a popular level.

To live subject to the Word is to confess our belief that the Lord is our guide, and he alone knows what we need. The life of the Church and the lives of Christians cannot be computer-programmed. It is a matter of letting oneself be lifted into the world of the Lord in order to be able to pour his love onto the whole human race.

Chapter 8

The *lectio divina* in the liturgy today: a key to pastoral renewal

John Glen

Pope John Paul II in a recent address to the Roman Clergy noted that one of the great blessings emanating from the Second Vatican Council was the provision of new categories and formulae in which to express the eternal truths of our faith for the men and women of our time. The Constitution on the Liturgy is a prime example. Even twenty-five years after its publication the Catholic community is still pondering the implications of its new categories within the liturgy.

The Council Fathers, for instance, emphasized the Trinitarian nature of the liturgy. The liturgy is the action of the Father, Son and Spirit in and through the whole People of God. This concept of the primordial Trinitarian nature of the liturgy has still to pervade the collective consciousness of the People of God. There remains, in some quarters, a misguided assumption that the liturgy is an activity restricted to the clergy.

Again, the Council Fathers stated that the liturgy, by its very nature, invites all the faithful to a full, conscious and active participation. In other words we come not to gape but to participate. The liturgy is a purposeful activity that flows out of our very hope, faith and love for God; it presupposes our Christian faith but at the same time nourishes that faith.

Likewise, the Constitution on the Liturgy recovers the traditional insight that the liturgy, by its very nature, is pastoral. The liturgy is one of the great sources of Christian growth and maturity; it is a well of living water to the Christian, not a show piece activity. Hence the Council Fa-

111

thers advocated the introduction of the mother tongue into the liturgy, in order that the words and actions of the liturgy should stimulate the minds and hearts of the faithful. The past twenty-five years have seen the liturgy of the Church being translated into an ever-increasing circle of mother tongues.

Notwithstanding all these category shifts, perhaps the most revolutionary of all the Council's insights into the nature of the liturgy was its perception of the scriptural nature of the liturgy. Of course the Church has always listened to and proclaimed the Word of God in the liturgy. Nevertheless, the revised Lectionary published in 1969 stands as a symbol of the direction that the Church wishes the liturgical reform to take into the next millennium. From this point onwards the Church envisages no liturgical celebration without a liturgical *lectio divina*.

Jesus Christ: God's lectio divina

This is not simply a disciplinary decision of the Council. Rather the Word of God is central to the very nature of the liturgy. The originality of the liturgy rests upon the originality of the message of salvation. In the liturgy we *celebrate* what God has done for the world in Jesus Christ. The first intimations of that divine activity are to be found in the Book of Genesis. Here the Christian people learn how universal is God's love; the whole of creation belongs to him, not just one little section of humanity, not just one golden epoch in history; God is always acting, always creating, crazily in love with his creation, present to men and women in the most intimate depths of their consciousness in the person of the Holy Spirit, the *Ruah Yahweh*.

But in the coming of Jesus Christ, the Son of God, born of Mary, the meaning of God's activity in the world becomes even more clear. For from the inner relationship between Jesus of Nazareth and God the Father is born the revelation of the purpose of that divine activity in creation; it is a knowledge, a revelation, that owes everything to the very nature of Jesus not simply as a Son of God, but, as St John expresses it, "the only Son of God". The mission and message of Jesus of Nazareth disclose that God invites all people to plunge into the stream of divine consciousness, divine love, to begin here and now to live eternal life, just as Jesus of Nazareth, the Christ, lived in conscious unity, inseparably united in mind and heart with his Father.

Jesus of Nazareth comes then not simply to disclose religious truths previously unknown to the human race. Jesus comes primarily to carry humanity across the threshold of suffering, pain and death into the experience of eternal life, resurrection, or into the immersion into the life of Father, Son and Spirit, in short, the Trinity.

The New Testament, then, is not simply a catalogue of events in the life of Jesus of Nazareth and the early Christian community. The authors have not used scissors and paste to stick together a record of happenings. The New Testament more than anything else charts a normative life of experience, the life experience of Jesus Christ, as the foundational experience of what it means for the human and the divine to be totally wrapped up in each other. When we see Jesus we see one who is perfectly in touch with God, totally obedient to the will of God, uniquely present to the Father as only "the only Son of God" can be. We see one who lives in the world in the heart of the Trinity.

Yet it remains a fact of life that the only Son of God came and lived in a particular socio-ethnic context in history. He who by nature was divine, emptied himself, assuming the condition of people in his day and age. He lived within the contours of a human consciousness unaccustomed to generators, pylons and electricity; there were no asphalt roads; in an age before Voyager II, and when everyone believed the world was flat, he would never have seen Neptune's magnificent storms. Nuclear power and science lay beyond his human consciousness.

It would be futile for men and women of today to seek answers to questions that arise out of a totally different human consciousness from the one inhabited by the men and women in the time of Jesus of Nazareth. His "world" was so different from our "world". But we do turn to Jesus to understand what it means to live totally in communion with God and totally obedient to the will of the Father. This is what is universal in the life of Christ and which stands as a model for all time. Christ's life stands as a normative structure, a normative recurring pattern, for the way in which God builds himself into the lives of individuals and the lives of nations. Hence it is imperative to know the Jesus story and for that story to be etched into our hearts: for as Jesus lives so must we.

Nothing in the life of Jesus is meaningless. From the very beginning of his public life he gathered a small band of disciples, sufficient in the Jewish tradition, to constitute a liturgical assembly. In this liturgical assembly was the Word of God; better, the liturgical assembly was constituted and brought into existence by the Word of God, Jesus Christ.

At no time, therefore, do we have any other picture of the Church than that of Jesus, the Word of God, dwelling in the midst of his followers. Indeed, one might say his followers are those who listen to his voice, walk and live in the presence of that voice, and follow its dictates no matter the cost. Here then is our first image of the Church, the Body in communion with the Trinity. It is a picture of a people listening to the Son of God, revealing out of the depths of his own intimate relationship with the Father the unique experience of love which is to be made accessible to all. It is a picture of the *lectio divina*.

On the other hand, the New Testament writers record not only the moments when Christ succeeded in conveying this insight to his close disciples, but also the many frustrating moments over three years. St Mark instances many moments when the disciples and the crowds failed to understand what was unfolding before their very eyes. For Christ's grasp of

God's activity in the affairs of men, though rooted in the Hebrew tradition, was radically different from that of the contemporary religious authorities. So radically different, in fact, that the religious authorities were convinced Jesus of Nazareth must be arrested, and put to death by the full might of the occupying Roman forces. St Matthew and St John document how seriously the Jewish religious leaders viewed the threat of Jesus of Nazareth; at risk was the very notion of God and the very understanding of God's relationship to the human race. Jesus was proclaiming a new understanding of God and thereby a new vision of humanity. It is a God who loves and loves and gives and gives; it is of men and women who can love and love and give and give when they are sealed in the love of the Trinity, the Spirit of Father and Son.

The disciples would have to wait until the resurrection of Jesus in order to understand the experience of the Holy Spirit, sealing and binding all who lived in him. It would take the force and conviction of this new experience of God and humanity to overthrow the ballast of their former interpretation of their religious experience. From now on the disciples in times of trouble or perplexity turned to that experience of God in their lives, the presence of the Spirit of the Risen One in their consciousness, to assist and guide them in discerning the will of God. The mission of the Son gives way to the mission of the Spirit. From now onwards the disciples will discern the will of God for all nations in faithful adherence to the twin "compass point" bearings of the normative life of Christ and the authentic responding to the Spirit of the Risen One in their hearts.

Jesus Christ, then, is the *lectio divina*, God's *lectio divina* to the world. But to read and understand his life, his mission and, above all, the significance of his death and resurrection, requires the gift of the Holy Spirit. The High Priest and the leaders of the Jewish people knew everything there was to know about Jesus of Nazareth; yet they were blind to everything he meant. To understand Jesus, we need the gift of the resurrection, the gift of his own Spirit, so that we might

115

understand him from within and from our experience of life in the Trinity.

The liturgy celebrates and nourishes this new understanding of how it is between us and God and between ourselves and each other. The liturgy points to a new way of living; it signals a new sense of identity, a new sense of consciousness which is recognizably that of Jesus Christ. That religious consciousness of Jesus Christ is normative for Christians of all ages. Hence whenever the Church celebrates the touching of that experience in the sacraments, so too the Church celebrates her understanding of that experience in her *lectio divina* for each of the sacraments.

The lectio divina:
  a key to understanding the sacraments

For example parents may bring their infants to the community to be baptized for a host of reasons. They may regard Baptism as a protection against evil, as an insurance that the child will wax good and strong, or as a social custom. But when the *lectio divina* takes place before Baptism, the Church's understanding of the meaning of the action is revealed, namely of being plunged into a whole experience of life which is based on the life, death and resurrection of Jesus Christ. The *lectio divina* reveals the Christian nature of Baptism; it reveals what the Church has conserved in her understanding through the Holy Spirit and what she is celebrating.

The more the baptismal *lectio divina* is taken seriously pastorally, the more it will become obvious many parents will need assistance with pre-Baptism programmes, in order to celebrate with the Church the Baptism of their child. The baptismal *lectio divina* provides them with the clue to what the Church is celebrating. In recent years there are signs that more and more parishes are responding to the voice of the Holy Spirit in this area.

116

Likewise, in the sacrament of Penance, restored in 1975, there is provision for a *lectio divina* in all forms of the celebration of the sacrament. Once again it is only when the *lectio divina* is taken seriously that the unique Christian meaning of the action is revealed. For when Christians come to celebrate this sacrament it is not simply to catalogue their faults and failures, nor to expunge their fears, phobias and repressions.

The motivation is not purely humanistic. The Church reveals through her *lectio divina* that the Christian comes to celebrate the Gospel forgiveness, the Gospel mercy and the Gospel peace of Jesus Christ in order to mediate that same forgiveness and mercy "to those who trespass against us". As we discover the depths of God's forgiveness for us, so too do we begin to tap the depths of forgiveness in ourselves for those who do us wrong.

Gradually the *lectio divina* is being incorporated into the pastoral practice of our parishes. In the communal forms of celebration the Word of God has become the standard by which we judge our lives. In the individual form of celebrating the sacrament of Penance, the integration of the *lectio divina* has taken somewhat longer. It is a new element for both priest and people. Yet experience has shown that over the fifteen years of its introduction the *lectio divina* has proved itself to be of inestimable worth to penitents and ministers alike.

Another, and at first sight a rather puzzling introduction of the *lectio divina* into the liturgy, has come with the new Rite for the Pastoral Care of the Sick and Dying. The Church's *lectio divina* for this sacrament radiates her faith, her hope and love of God in times of sickness and death. Inevitably at such times the sick person and the friends and relatives agonize over the meaning of pain and suffering. The *lectio divina* seeks not to explain away suffering and death but points to the experience of Jesus and the manner in which he embraced his own suffering and death on the cross.

When parishes can celebrate this sacrament in homes,

hospitals, and even in the parish church, then the *lectio divina* becomes an integral and uplifting moment for the sick, their family and friends and the whole parish community.

As Ordinations come to be celebrated more and more in the parishes people are hearing the Church's *lectio divina* for deacons, priests and bishops. For the candidates of Ordination these wonderful scriptural texts come as no surprise. They represent the normative, enduring understanding of the Church with regard to Ordination in the Church. Young men come with their own models of priesthood and diaconate at the beginning of their training.

It takes time for them to absorb the *lectio divina* into their lives; it demands much soul-searching to attune their desire to the Church's understanding of Ordination, the total gift of self to the Lord, head and members. The proclamation of the Word in the sacrament of Ordination, the liturgical lectio divina, trumpets the Church's grasp of the mystery of Ordination to candidates and community alike.

Similarly, in the sacrament of Matrimony, it is the *lectio divina* which provides the key to the Church's understanding of marriage. Marriage is, of course, a secular reality; the shape and forms of the institution of marriage differ from continent to continent, from epoch to epoch. In Ancient Roman society marriage was contractual. This meant that slaves could not marry since they were the property of their masters and thereby incapable of entering into contracts. Slaves could form liaisons but any children issuing from the liaison enjoyed no rights in law. Times change and so does the understanding of marriage in any given society.

When our young people ask to be married, more often than not, they are extremely influenced by the prevailing attitudes to marriage in society. That is why more and more parishes are insisting on couples attending pre-marriage courses. Here the Church's *lectio divina* can be placed before the couples, for not only society but the People of God has its own vision of marriage. It is of a relationship that mirrors the relationship between Christ and the Church; it is of a way of life that embraces the cross as well as the joy of the resurrection; it is of a sealing in love, a sealing in grace, so that faith, hope and love might abound. For the People of God marriage is not simply a secular reality; it is a spiritual one too, a way of life that draws people closer into the intimacy of the Trinity.

For the broad mass of Catholics, however, the principal experience of the liturgical *lectio divina* is the weekly Sunday Mass. For over twenty-five years now, in Britain, we have been listening to the Word of God proclaimed Sunday after Sunday in our own mother tongue. We have slowly been finding ways of celebrating the *lectio divina* of the Church; parishes meditate upon the First Reading by singing a psalm, an appropriate chant or song; the Gospel book is carried to the place of proclamation accompanied by Alleluias or Acclamations.

We are all, even if slowly, learning how to *celebrate* the *lectio divina* of the Mass. People are beginning to learn the skills of listening to the proclamation of the Word in a public place, with children present, and the inevitable coughing and scraping of chairs. People are beginning to expect a homily that targets the meaning of the Scripture readings or the prayers onto daily life in this part of the world. Catholic people are, through the liturgical *lectio divina*, being encouraged to deepen their understanding of God's Word.

In more and more parishes Bible Study groups and Prayer Groups are mushrooming. Catholics are gradually becoming more and more a people of the Word. But the impetus is arising out of the liturgical *lectio divina*. Only a deep love of the Word of God will prevent the *lectio divina* of the Mass sliding into dull, routine and grindingly predictable decline, or on the other hand spiralling into triviality. The liturgical *lectio divina* of the Mass is the principal experience of the Word of God for most young Catholics; that is why its celebration Sunday after Sunday requires creativity and imagination, in order that they can grasp and be grasped by the power of the Word of God, by the originality of the Gospel and the person of Jesus Christ.

Pastoral difficulties and challanges

In spite of the fact that the Vatican Council has made the liturgical *lectio divina* of the Church accessible to all, a number of difficulties continue to impede the full implementation of the Council's desire.

First, as Her Majesty's Inspectors of Schools point out, not everybody, even after compulsory schooling, has an adequate grasp of the English language. Likewise our parishes contain many people for whom English is a second language. This makes the proclamation of the Word at Mass less than effective. In the same way, when it comes to reading the Word of God at home, the modern conditions of life in this country are often unfavourable to quietly meditating upon the Word of God.

Then again there is an immediate cultural gap between the world of the Bible and the modern world of today. The common sense and outlook on life of the people in the Bible is so different from our modern outlook. From Genesis to the Apocalypse people think of the world in terms of Babylonian, Egyptian and Greek science. They talk of the sun standing still, waters up in the heavens, waters under the earth, heaven above and hell below. Our modern models of science give us a totally different picture of the world, one in which this earth is not the centre of the universe but one planet within a whole galaxy of solar systems.

At first sight the problem seems insoluble at a pastoral level. The biblical and the contemporary worlds appear to be poles apart. Yet appearances deceive, for while there are obvious dissimilarities between the two worlds of meaning there are also obvious similarities. For the author of Genesis, though operating out of a model of natural science different from the one we hold today, believed that God created the whole world and everything within it, that he is the God of everyone and not just interested in a particular segment of humanity or a particular epoch in human history; so too today do we believe.

Just as Paul, though operating with a different cosmology from ours today, believed that because of the resurrection of Christ the world was entering upon a decisive phase of its history, so too today do we believe. Likewise, just as the author of the Apocalypse believed that not only the past and the present lie in the hand of God but also the future destiny of the world, so too today do we believe.

The key then to understanding the world of the Bible is to be found in the use of analogy. For the Bible is not primarily a progress report on the history of science but the story of *God and humanity* acting together purposefully in time and space. The Bible interprets the hand of God in and through the hands of men and women; it tells of a Providence that is constructively and at times destructively present in the human condition, a Providence that reveals the meaning and purpose of life decisively in the life and mission of Jesus Christ.

That same story of God and humanity continues today and will continue till the end of time. God is always acting *today*. The apostles continued with the same method, taking the Scriptures and showing how they confirmed that God was acting in Jesus Christ *today*, "this Jesus whom you have crucified, he is Christ the Lord". Christians have a privileged perception into understanding God's activity in the world. They have the life of Christ. The more they are plunged into that life, steeped in and carried along by that life of Christ, the more will they too understand the hand and the will of God in their lives.

That is why the homily or the sermon forms an integral part of every liturgical lectio divina, because it points to where God is acting *now*. The great commentaries of the Patristic period are a reminder to us today of the importance the preaching bishops of those times accorded to the homily. Augustine, Basil, John Chrysostom, Gregory and Leo the

Great, Ambrose, John of Damascus all testify to the need for the *lectio divina* to be commented upon for *this group of people at this moment in time.* For what is at issue is where and how God is acting in our lives today.

By the time of the early Middle Ages these sermons in written form had become the basis of a whole tradition of understanding the activity of God in human history. Yet to St Thomas Aquinas and others a problem was posed not only by the vast quantity of commentaries but also by the many, varied and at times contradictory, opinions of the Fathers as to how God acts in our lives.

To tackle this difficulty of conflicting opinions among the Fathers, the mediaeval scholars introduced a new procedure. It was the question-and-answer method. They would gather together all the texts upon a topic, consistent and inconsistent alike, and attempt to detect whether there was a constant thread of meaning which was being carried forward across the different contexts and centuries.

The early mediaeval scholars were not content simply to compile former opinions; they sought to understand the underlying flow of the opinions of the Fathers, in order that they might present that understanding in a new and imaginative manner to the men and women *of their own time.* The genius of the early mediaeval scholars consisted in translating the biblical meaning, via the commentaries of the Fathers, into the new world context of their own mediaeval civilization.

In other words, they took the *lectio divina* of the Church as it had been understood through the patristic period and stimulated their own world with the freshness and vitality of that *understanding.* Sadly, in later centuries, when understanding ceased to play its vital role, the People of God became more and more estranged from the *lectio divina* not only by the use of Latin in the liturgy but also by a commentary tradition that prized moral exhortations, catechism formulae and rhetorical excellence.

In our own day Pope John Paul II is reviving the ancient

tradition of linking the *lectio divina* with an up-to-date relevant commentary. His commentary on the Book of Genesis is a valuable contribution to set alongside the commentaries of the great preaching bishops of the past. It serves also as an inspiration to all bishops and priests today to link the Church's understanding of the *lectio divina* with the best understanding of the problems and concerns of the contemporary world.

The key to gripping the minds and hearts of our contemporaries lies in our grasp of analogy, of being able to take the concrete demands of the Gospel, set in the world of Jesus Christ, and present them concretely before men and women in the twentieth century. To do this systematically and consistently means that one has *understood* the central insights of the Gospel, the essential truths of the Gospel as distinct from the cultural trappings in which they were originally cast. After that, it means also the ability to cast those insights and truths into the particular idioms and expressions of culture that make up the present world of our contemporaries. The world of the Bible is earthy, concrete, colourful and imaginative; the world of today is the same. In her poetry, art, music and language the Catholic Church all over the world is trying to forge new ways of bringing the essential message of the *lectio divina* to men and women living in and moving swiftly into a new epoch of human history. The Second Vatican Council has given us everything we need in order to respond to that challenge: the *lectio divina*, proclaimed in the public assembly, applied to contemporary life, meditated upon and assimilated in the tranquillity of private prayer.

The Christian today, however, is comforted by the fact that the building of a new epoch in human history is primarily the work of the Spirit of Jesus, working in his Church, but also mysteriously and anonymously in the minds and hearts of all men and women of goodwill. In other words the modern Catholic is from the outset ecumenical in attitude, open to discerning, affirming and following the impulses of the Spirit of the Risen One in both the Church and the world. There can be no such thing nowadays as an unecumenical Catholic. That would be to deny the mission of the Spirit, the *fides ex infusione.*

Nonetheless, Catholics believe that all the goodwill, the grace, the joy, the endeavour which the Spirit raises in the lives of everyone, finds its focus, its inspiration in the knowledge of Christ Jesus and in the grace and fellowship of his Church. Hence the importance in today's world of the proclamation of the Word, for a *fides ex auditu,* in other words, the importance of the *lectio divina.* Young people today need to know the Gospel roots of all that is good and noble in life. Without a sustained programme of *lectio divina,* a new generation will lose the focus, Jesus Christ, for those inner aspirations of freedom, peace, joy, love, fellowship and transpose them into other channels and directions. There are signs in Western Europe at least that such a process is already under way. That is why the *lectio divina* in the liturgy and the pastoral life of parishes is so important nowadays. Without it a whole new generation is in grave risk of losing its sense of direction in life, of trivializing life itself, of declining into cynicism and despair.

For this reason the Catholic community of today and tomorrow is becoming more and more the radical alternative for those increasingly disillusioned with the secular vision of life. There is much that is wrong with both the Church and society but in the Church there is always the *lectio divina* to assist in detecting the hand of God, the will of God, and so arresting the process of decline.

That is why, over the years, Christians come gradually to treasure the *lectio divina* of the Church. We are all coming to love hearing the Last Supper narrative on Maundy Thursday, the Passion narrative of St John on Good Friday, the Easter narratives on Easter Sunday, the Advent and Christmas readings, the readings for Baptism, Marriage, Funerals. These readings are fast becoming not simply a call to conversion, the upbuilding of our faith, but quite simply our delight. Like a grandfather listening to the sounds of the voices of the children playing, so are we beginning just to love hearing the sound of the *lectio divina* in the liturgy and in our prayer.

The Christian life is one of strife, living in the teeth of opposition a life of achievement. Yet the Christian life is also quite simply a life of deep contentment, reminiscent of the original contentment when man and woman, *ish* and *ishah*, walked hand in hand with God in the cool of the garden.

The *lectio divina* helps us find the hand of God. When we put our hand in his hand and listen to his voice in the *lectio divina*, then indeed, even in this life, we are enjoying the intimacy of love heralded by Jesus Christ, the intimacy of the Trinity.

Bibliography

Barclay W., *Crucified and Crowned*, SMC 1961

Barrett C.K., *The Gospel according to St John*, SPCK 1956

Bligh J., *The Sign of the Cross*, St Paul Publications, Slough 1974

Bloom A., *Meditations on a Theme*, Mowbrays 1972

Bornkamm G., *Tradition and Interpretation in Matthew*, SCM 1982

Breemen P.G., *As Bread that is Broken*, Dimension 1974

Brown R.E., *The Critical Meaning of the Bible*, G. Chapman 1981
– *The Birth of the Messiah*, G. Chapman 1977
– *The Gospel according to John*, Anchor Bible, Doubleday 1966 and G. Chapman 1971

Brown R.E./Fitzmyer J.A./Murphy R.E. (eds.), *Jerome Biblical Commentary*, G. Chapman 1981

Charlier C., *The Christian Approach to the Bible*, Sands 1957

Cooper R., *The Gospel according to Mark*, Arnold 1988
– *The Gospel according to Luke*, Arnold 1989

Cox D., *The Psalms in the Life of God's People*, St Paul Publications, Slough 1984
– *Man's anger and God's silence: the book of Job*, St Paul Publications, Slough 1990

Dalrymple J., *The Longest Journey*, DLT 1979

Deiss L., *Biblical Prayers*, World Library 1976

Dodd C.H., *The Fourth Gospel*, CUP 1980

Drury J., *The Parables in the Gospels*, SPCK 1986
– *Tradition and Design in Luke's Gospel*, DLT 1976

Fitzmyer J.A., *The Gospel according to Luke*, Doubleday 1983

Gibbard M., *Prayer and Contemplation*, Mowbrays 1976

Jeremias J., *Rediscovering the Parables*, SCM 1966

Johnson W., *The Inner Eye of Love*, Fount 1978

Koch K., *The Book of Books*, SCM 1968

Maertens T., *Biblical Themes*, Biblica 1964

Marshall I.H., *The Gospel of St Luke*, Paternoster Press 1978

Martin R.P., *New Testament Foundations*, Eerdmans 1975

McKenzie J.L., *Dictionary of the Bible*, G. Chapman 1965

McLoughlin V., *Reading in Church*, Mayhew-McCrimmon 1976

Megivern J.J., *Bible Interpretation*, Consortium 1978

Schökel L.A., *Understanding Biblical Research*, Burns & Oates 1968

Schweizer E., *The Good News according to Matthew*, SPCK 1975

Shorter A., *Revelation and its Interpretation*, G.Chapman 1983

Toal M.F., *Sunday Sermons of the Great Fathers*, vols 1-3, Longman 1959